Managing People in Organisations

Managing People in Organisations

The Challenges of Change

B.R. VIRMANI

Response Books
A division of Sage Publications
New Delhi/Thousand Oaks/London

Copyright © B.R. Virmani, 2000

First published in 2000 by

Response Books
A division of Sage Publications India Pvt Ltd
M–32, Greater Kailash Market I
New Delhi 110 048

Sage Publications Inc
2455 Teller Road
Thousand Oaks, California 91320

Sage Publications Ltd
6 Bonhill Street
London EC2A 4PU

Published by Tejeshwar Singh for Response Books, lasertypeset by Line Arts, Pondicherry and printed at Chaman Enterprises, Delhi.

Library of Congress Cataloging-in-Publication Data
Virmani, B.R.
    Managing people in organisations: the challenges of change/B.R. Virmani.
      p. cm.   (C)
    Includes bibliographical references and index.
    1. Personnel management—India. 2. Personnel management. 3. Manpower planning—India. I. Title.
HF5549.2.I4 V57   2000   658.3'00954—dc21   00–028278

ISBN: 0–7619–9447–5 (US-HB)   81–7036–904–5 (India-HB)

Production Team: Seetha Parthasarathy, O.P. Bhasin, and Santosh Rawat

To the memory of
Ashish
*whose interest in management was nipped in
the bud by cruel fate while he was a student
at BITS, Pilani.*

Contents

Introduction

With growing globalisation, the accent has gradually shifted from the legal and welfare approach to viewing the human resource function as a tool for the development of the total human resources in the organisation to meet the challenge of competition. The rapid technological changes have also necessitated this. As a consequence of the economic liberalisation in India, there has been tremendous pressure on the government as well as business enterprises to improve their competitive capabilities. Gearing up to the emerging opportunities and staying in a competitive environment requires greater responsibility and innovative approaches than have been evident so far. There is also a need for a strong element of professionalisation in managing and developing human resources. All these require an understanding of the strategic dimension of various policies and practices that have a bearing on human resource planning, development and management.

Lately, human resource management (HRM) and human resource development (HRD) have been considered as important approaches to the management of an organisation in a wide range of competitive economies. The original 19th and 20th century British and, subsequently, the American model of managing human resources and governing the employer–employee relationship became popular in India and was absorbed in a wide variety of organisational settings. However, with changes in the overall economic scenario and the technology, there is need to relook and redefine some of the traditional HRM practices. This calls for a much wider discussion and debate on the nature of HRM, its sources, operation, philosophy, etc. Even some of the western economies like the UK or USA which once seem to enjoy a distinctive and successful pattern of HRM have been attracted to the debate as they, specially Britain, have been struggling with problematic industrial relations and even low growth.

Two related themes run through this book. Both are concerned with the nature of HRM. The first relates to the macro-level antecedents of HRM in India and abroad specially in western countries, and its transplantation in other economies with particular emphasis on India, where recently there has been a vibrant HRM debate involving practitioners and academics alike. There are many unresolved questions regarding the model of HRM that can be adopted in the Indian context, such as: What sort of example of HRM are we setting? Can it be transferred from one economy to another? Are its policies and practices internationally applicable? Do HRM policies contribute to strategic management? The types of questions raised in relation to HRM indicate the extent to which it has disturbed many formally accepted concepts, especially those relating to employer–employee relationships.

The other theme relates to the organisational context in which HRM has emerged and operates. This context is not simply a set of operational matters that describe the functional role of personnel management, but a complex process that helps us understand the nature of organisational life and the role of human resources in meeting strategic challenges. The purpose of this book is to present an analysis of these relationships in terms of contemporary HRM debate. Many books in the area of HRM emphasise the traditional analysis of personnel management or industrial relations starting from selection, recruitment to disciplinary measures. However, this book starts with the nature of management issues, especially those related to HRM, in the Indian context, cross-cultural issues, the conflict with foreign management concepts. It then extends the analysis to some key areas of HRM and HRD as a means of stimulating discussion on the issues affecting the management of people in the contemporary competitive situation.

There are few books which attempt to critically analyse and debate some of the traditional or even current HRM practices at both the strategic and international level, and which, at the same time, provide an easy access to these debates for the layman. This book attempts to bridge this important gap. The objective of this book is to provide, in a simple and easily acceptable form, some of the major developments in the field of HRM in the context of recent changes in the global environment, combined with some explanation as to how internationally accepted HRM concepts can be transplanted in the Indian environment. This by no means is an easy task. The difficulty in achieving this balance continues to be a major concern for management practitioners and academicians and making their human resource management practices and policies relevant, applicable and academically sound. This book can help to provide certain guidelines to management practitioners, policy makers and students of management.

A distinguishing feature of this book is that most of the chapters are based on first-hand research, case studies and data collection done over the last decade. All this raises, in some cases, fundamental issues about HRM and the employer–employee relationship. The case studies are designed to encourage practitioners and students to draw certain lessons and apply the knowledge gained. This does not imply that there is a single perspective which dominates either the book or the human resource function. What unites all the chapters is the underlying theme that HRM and HRD require a rational analysis rather than blindly following traditional models and practices; the fact that many traditional practices of HRM have been adopted by organisations demands that they are systematically examined from a variety of different standpoints. The main themes covered in the book are in the following pattern.

Most of the HRM practices in India have been borrowed from the West. These often clashed with the Indian value system and environment. This led to some workable solutions being found but they, in turn, conflicted with western management theories.

There is also pressure to rapidly industrialise and compete in a liberalised global environment, primarily on the western model. Support facilities have been created to train and develop management personnel to administer the whole apparatus. Modelled on western education, Indian universities and institutes have formulated courses in management to meet the demands for qualified managerial personnel. The Indian manager today, educated either in the West or tutored in western management literature attempts to manage and administer the Indian industrial structure on western principles. This, he finds, does not work. Compromises result, often accompanied by frustration. Work does not proceed as planned. Goals are, however, achieved. Management is 'somehow' effected.

There is a distinct hiatus between the professed policies and the practices followed in the Indian environment as a result of these compromises. Assuming that foreign management practices will work equally well in Indian conditions, policies are evolved and plans made. Since goals set in this way are largely achieved, there is a perception that management practices in India are similar to the foreign ones. This may not be always true. Our study of Indian management practices shows that they are quite different from western practices.

The socio-cultural environment in India is unique. Its peculiarities mould the personality of the management practitioners and influence management practice which is different from the professed principles. The first chapter deals with this gap between the professed principles and actual practices. It also attempts to find out the factors that influence HRM practices and decision making in the Indian environment; and, finally, how people perceive management. Some indicators are also provided about the direction in which Indian management is heading.

The traditional model of personnel management is characterised by the notion that labour is a cost factor that has to be controlled and contained. In these circumstances, employees become one of the aggregate commodities within the organisation that have to be managed within the organisation's resources in the same way that, say, finance is managed. The logical extension of this model is reached in manpower planning with precise numerical assessment of the internal and external demand for supply of labour.

Any alternative approach which treats the individual as a resource rather than an expense and views expenditure on development of employees as an investment, rather than cost is at times perceived as a threat to conventional theory of personnel management. The advent of Japanese management systems, however, has highlighted the impact of treating expenditure on human resource as an investment and not a cost. Whether sustainable in India or not, the Japanese concept, which emphasises on developing individual employees along particular job paths while assuring continuous employment throughout the individual's working life, has at least provided a model in which the employer seeks to maximise employment opportunities. This approach goes further however, and regards all employees as potentially able to benefit from further training and development, from which the organisation itself then benefits. So, far from viewing the employee as a cost, this philosophy sees the employee as an actual and potential return on investment that ultimately strengthens the organisation. The responsibility of the employer for investment and employment has, to an extent, encouraged large corporate Japanese employers to develop products and markets which have used the invested skills of their workforce.

In India there has been a resurgence of interest in the importance of human resource. There is now a greater awareness of the investment potential in training and development of the human resources. This has been expressed in terms of the relatively poor record in industrial and occupational training as a function of investment. Thus, HRM has brought to prominence a concern for maximising the potential of employees which traditional personnel management theory did not address.

Chapter 2 addresses in detail, the question of how one can go about planning for HRD, especially upgradation of the skills and knowledge of the employees. It also discusses various issues connected with technological change and the need for developing employment and redeployment strategies.

Chapter 3 discusses how organisations can link their corporate strategy with training and development of the human resources in the organisation. During the last two decades there has been greater awareness regarding management training and development in all the sectors of Indian economy. As a result, there has been a growing need to find ways and means to improve the - efficiency and effectiveness of management training and development activity from the point of view of the organisation. However, in spite of this, there has been very little systematic emphasis on evaluation. To fill this gap, a longitudinal study of management training and development and its evaluation was undertaken in Indian organisations. The research study was divided into two phases. The first phase dealt with the transfer of learning in the training context and the second phase related to transfer of learning to the job. Chapters 4 and 5 look at the findings of the study and also suggest a broad framework of the evaluation model to make training and development more effective in the organisational context.

Chapter 6 discusses the issue of management education and training in the changing environment as, in many cases, training has degenerated into a fad without any substantive benefit to the organisation. The chapter deals with the role of the training institutions, the training/HRD managers and the areas of possible research to make management education and training more effective in the fast changing Indian environment.

There has been a constant debate about the efficacy of technical institutions to prepare personnel to meet the fast changing technological environment in the organisations. A large number of organisations have evolved their own engineer trainee schemes. However, certain doubts have been expressed about the efficient functioning of such schemes in terms of meeting the needs of technological change. Chapter 7 deals with the various issues connected with the development of the technical trainee schemes and also makes certain suggestions to improve such schemes at the organisation level. The chapter is based on the findings of a study conducted in association with the Federation of Indian Chambers of Commerce and Industry (FICCI) comprising 90 organisations in India.

The past decade has witnessed a phenomenal change, especially with the collapse of communism and the break-up of the erstwhile USSR. Economic barriers between various nations are being steadily dismantled specially after the signing of the General Agreement on Tariffs and Trade (GATT). There is an increasing free flow of goods, services and manpower. At the same time, regional economic blocs are also being formed. There is an increasing pressure on industry to meet the demands of a competitive environment.

In India the major investment in terms of HRD and training is in the supervisory and managerial cadre. But more than 80 per cent of the workforce comprises the workers. Little organised effort has gone in towards workers' education and training, though the Government of India had set up a Central Board for Workers Education in 1948 with regional centres all over the country. Many questions have been raised about the efficacy of workers' education schemes. Chapter 8 deals with the study of the functioning of workers' education schemes and the relevant issues and problems and suggests a different model that can be adopted at the national as well as the organisational level to educate and continually train the workers.

Technology has played a crucial role in enhancing competitiveness. With the emergence of transnational corporations (TNCs) and multinational corporations (MNCs), technology is no longer confined to a particular country. Some countries, however, cannot afford to develop their own technologies. They, therefore, seek technology from TNCs and MNCs. However, some mutually beneficial conditions should be attached before any transfer of technology takes place. Also there is an important issue of capacity of the newly developed and developing countries to not only attract new technologies but also develop the capabilities of their human resources to absorb, assimilate and further develop technology. Closely linked to these issues are the economic policies of individual countries and the business environment and infrastructure they need to provide for both domestic and external investments in technology development and upgradation. Human resources play a crucial role in not only the transfer, but also the assimilation and further development, of technology.

Some countries in the Asian region have, in the last two decades, successfully developed their economies and achieved some of the highest growth rates in the world. However, lately they have faced an economic crisis. On the other hand, countries like India, which are also at the threshold of development, are still searching for appropriate models of growth.

Chapters 9 and 10 discuss the issues connected with globalisation, technological change, HRM and HRD. They also give some comparative analysis of a few Asian countries such as Singapore, Malaysia and Thailand. With the help of the case studies from Indian organisations it is seen that for appropriate technology transfer, assimilation and development, the emphasis on upgradation of human resources is crucial. Certain guidelines have been provided as to how an organisation and its human resources can be prepared for technological change.

The industrial relations system is normally perceived as one of the rules and regulations that govern the relationship between the employers and employees. Different parties connected with the industrial relations system have evolved this institutionalised structure over the years. These parties are the employers and the hierarchy of managers; the workers and their spokesmen; and government agencies concerned with workers.

As these rules were originally set solely by the employers and society perceived these rules as being exploitative of workers, the government was compelled to protect the workers. There was a simultaneous and gradual movement towards unity among the workers, culminating in the emergence of trade unions which became a tool of collective resistance by the workers. This gave birth to bipartism and collective bargaining became a means of setting the rules and terms of co-operation between the employees and the employers. Gradually, the institution of collective bargaining developed its own features so as to maintain a balance of power between the actors concerned, laying primary emphasis on the non-sharing of full information, leading to mistrust and hence to other pressure tactics.

Collective bargaining still continues to be one of the important institutions for regulating the industrial relations system. However, during the last three decades, there have been far reaching changes in the economic scenario, having a major impact on industry and its pattern of investment. The institution of collective bargaining was based on class conflict and an adversarial approach with the premise that the proprietor is the owner and master, who has a tendency to exploit and there have to be countervailing forces to prevent such exploitation. However, the whole concept of owner and servant needs re-definition as in today's environment, it is difficult to determine who is the real owner. In a public enterprise all are employees and even the top management could be termed as servants. In private enterprises also there may be marginal investment by the owners themselves as most of the funds are borrowed from public sources. The stake of the so-called owners in the enterprise is marginal and thus, in most cases, they are the managers rather than the owners of the enterprise. Therefore, the old concept of adversarial relationship and consequent collective bargaining is becoming irrelevant. There are also other interest groups like consumers and the shareholders. Therefore, it is very difficult in today's scenario to determine who is exploiting whom and who is whose adversary.

Chapter 11 discusses the changing industrial relations scenario. The impact of collective bargaining has been detailed with help of some case studies and alternative approaches to the theory of HRM and industrial relations have been suggested. Reference is also made to the need for change in the company laws which, again, is based on the traditional 19th century British model which does not distinguish between a small and a large limited liability company, nor between nationalised industries and other companies covered under legislation. There may be a need for some fundamental changes in the company law. In a changing environment, the role of the trade unions, the management, government and the academicians is also discussed.

The ultimate focus of any HRM or HRD in the organisational context involves preparing people and organisations for change, which requires deliberate action steps to bring about change. Different firms in the oil and petroleum sector in India have been experimenting with transformation and change through development of corporate strategies and networking, even though at times they are market rivals. Chapter 12 details the unique experiment being attempted by these companies in preparing themselves for global competition, with special focus on preparing their human resources, not only to increase their capabilities, but also to bring about a change in the mindset. This strategic model of the change process can be applied in any large organisation or group of organisations.

B.R. Virmani

Acknowledgements

- Mr Sunil Unny Guptan who was a member of the team for research on Indian management practices and also my co-author of the book on this subject.
- Friedrich Ebert Foundation, Bonn and New Delhi, which partly funded the research work on Technology Transfer, HRD aspects and Workers' Education, and also helped in the presentation of my paper on Redefining Industrial Relations, along with the Shri Ram Centre for Industrial Relations and Human Resources, Delhi.
- Dr Vinayshil Gautam of Indian Institute of Technology, Delhi, for organising a seminar on management research where my paper on Management Education and Training in the Changing Environment was originally presented.
- Dr Premila Verma who was a member of the team for research on evaluation of training and development and my co-author of the book on the subject.
- The Federation of Indian Chambers of Commerce and Industry (FICCI) which originally partly funded my work on Developing Technical Training Schemes.
- Mr U.K. Dikshit and Dr Anjali Hazarika of the National Petroleum Management Programme (NPMP), New Delhi for necessary

support in terms of organising a series of programmes for the petroleum and related sectors in India and thus contributing to the chapter on Managing Transformation: Indian Initiatives in Organisation Change through Networking—Case of the Oil Sector.

- Indian Society for Training and Development (ISTD), New Delhi, which first published the original article on Managing Transformation and which has been revised for this book.
- Mr T.L. Sankar, Principal, Administrative Staff College of India (ASCI), Hyderabad for providing necessary support for collection of data and for updating of some of the articles in this book.
- Dr C.S. Venkata Ratnam, Dean, International Management Institute, New Delhi, for his useful comments and suggestions.
- Indian Petro-Chemicals Corporation Limited (IPCL), especially its Chairman and Managing Director, Mr K.G. Ramanathan, who supported the study by instituting the Chair Professorship at ASCI that was held by me.
- Mr H.K. Srinivas, for his help in collecting case data and in preparation of the paper on the oil sector in India.
- Last but not the least, Ms Edna John at ASCI, and Ms N. Sujatha and Mr M. Srikanth at the Centre for Organisation Research and Development in Management (CORD-M) for their secretarial, administrative and editorial assistance.

BRV

1

Management in India—The Cultural Dilemmas

Most management practices in India have been borrowed from the West due to historical reasons. However, they clash with the Indian value system, creating problems within organisations. Some workable solutions are found, sometimes on a day-to-day basis and at other times on a sustained basis. However, these are not in consonance with management theory originating in the West. Recently, there has been a lot of talk about Indian concepts of management. But there is a lack of clarity about these concepts and how they can be translated into institutional structures. Some theorists talk of personalised leadership styles, more as a manipulative device; others talk of the Japanese style of group decision-making. However, it is difficult to adopt them in organisations because of the dominance of western management concepts.

Management concepts in the West evolved in a particular socio-cultural milieu and adapted themselves to political and economic changes. This process of evolution did not happen in India. It was found convenient to borrow human resources technology just as one acquires scientific technology. As a result of this grafting process, there is some confusion in management thinking.

Of late, there has been greater mobility of skilled personnel, a widespread demand for shared decision-making, increasing demands from customers for quality products and the assimilation of so-called modern techniques and methods of organisation for managerial effectiveness. But the limitations have to be borne in mind that some elements of culture are more responsive to change than others. Thus, when many Indian managers are exposed to modern western management principles and techniques, the social environment affects their perception and assimilation of new knowledge. So while they are convinced about its usefulness, they do not really implement it.

The Indian Experience

In India, there are different kinds of organisation cultures: the traditional family-run firms; public sector enterprises; government departments; and MNCs. They adopt different kinds of managerial practices, but find these difficult to apply. They, therefore, try to evolve some workable systems of management.

The Indian environment is characterised by a strong sense of tradition or *parampara*. Respect for age is taken as assumed. The feeling of security inherent in the joint family tradition is sought even in the workplace, encouraging a paternalistic environment. The Hindu concept of the cyclic nature of time, with life being a series of births and rebirths, leads to a fixation on *karma*—a sense that everything is preordained.

It is with this background that modern India is attempting rapid industrialisation on the western model, leapfrogging the period of transition. Support facilities have been created to train management personnel to administer the system. Indian universities and institutes have, on the lines of institutes in the West, formulated courses in management disciplines to meet the demands for qualified managerial personnel.

Along with the technology transfer, there is always a tendency to transfer managerial systems and practices in the belief that western management concepts are universal. However, such grafting does not always work. In such situations, organisations attempt compromises which leads to a divergence between the professed policies and actual practice in the local environment.[1] However, goals set by this measure are largely achieved. Hence, the popular perception that management practices in India are also like the foreign ones. This, however, is an illusion. The real practices in the Indian industrial set-up are quite different.

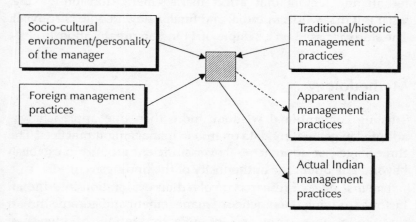

This graphic representation expresses the situation that Indian management is in. The supplanting of alien management practices into the Indian situation has various 'forces' that bear on its implementation. The socio-cultural environment of the managers, who are the instruments of the practice of management, is expressed through their personality traits. Added to this are the management practices that have been followed through the ages. These 'forces' influence the management practices in the Indian environment. Consequently, there is a difference between the management practices that actually take place and what is projected as taking place.[2]

There are two reasons for the discrepancy between apparent management practices and the actual management practices. One, in order to make things work, certain compromises are made in the principles and policies. They are not strictly followed while parts of them are given the go-by. Two, it is often believed that 'since the goals have been achieved, the policies must be working'. To admit otherwise is to renounce much of what is learnt in business schools and to recant what has been professed over the years.

This chapter attempts to probe the gaps in Indian management—between the actual practices and the apparent ones as projected by the policies; to find out what are the distinct and differentiating factors that affect management decision-making; what is it that works in India; and finally, how people perceive it. The study is based on a sample of 44 Indian organisations.

Methodology

Trusting conventional wisdom, more than one approach was adopted in generating data on Indian management practices. The three stages, or approaches, cover sufficient ground to establish beyond any doubt the authenticity of the findings.

The *first stage* of research involved an exploration into Indian history, studying the practice of management and administration through the ages—from ancient India, through the Middle Ages, the Mughals, the British, and finally, 'modern management' in India. To serve as a comparison, a parallel is also sought in the evolution of management outside India.

The *second step* of the research involved in-depth, semi-structured interviews with 86 persons. The participants in the study came from 44 organisations and represented diverse functions and hierarchical levels ranging from workers and chief executives in the corporate sector to ministers in the central government. The organisations covered were the public sector undertakings at the central and the state levels; private sector—both MNCs and family-owned; government ministries; and financial institutions.

The *third stage* of data collection was an in-depth study of four organisations in India, each representative of different types of establishments: a government department, an MNC with foreign participation in equity, a traditional family-managed private sector company, and a public sector undertaking.

Management in Ancient India

The period known as ancient India or the Hindu period has been systematically recorded by thinkers and writers of the time as well as foreign travellers. The ancient Hindu scriptures, the Vedas tried to codify the state's affairs and the organisation of the people, their lifestyle and culture. They also provide indicators about the system of administration in vogue. This system was tied closely to the existing social practice of the *varna* or the caste system.[3] Each participant in the social process—from the king to the lowest man—had his or her 'duties', expected role and behaviour set out. Administration revolved around the king as the head of the clans.

Historically, the birth of Indian organisations started with the family, its head and then possibly extended to the clan, the tribe and the king. For thousands of years, the family head, the chief or the king always played a dominant role in the ultimate decision-making process. Still, there is also evidence to indicate that there was a tradition of consultation by the head and certain checks and balances were present to ensure that justice was done. For example, during the Vedic period (B.C. 1700–1200) there was a strict written code of conduct laid down in the Vedas where duties of the king, the heads and the subjects were stipulated. Any deviation from these was considered a sin.

The advent of modern organisations started with the development of the guild. Artisans practising a particular trade organised themselves into a common guild and selected their own head. The king also regulated the functioning of the guilds to ensure that no member is exploited.

One striking feature of Indian management in those times was the role of the extended family. Along with incentives, rewards and punishment, there was a certain amount of built-in security for the members. However, independent of this security which the family/guild provided to its members, they were also expected to obey the authority which was linked to age and the principle of seniority. There were periods when both these principles were tampered with by foreign invaders but these deviations could not last long because of the deep-rooted attachment to traditional values.

This reliance on family/blood ties resulted in outsiders being viewed with mistrust, no matter how efficient they were. Therefore, no outsider or external agency was allowed. At the same time, there was infighting within family. This is true of today's administration also, whether in an enterprise or at the national level. There may be still a preference for caste, religion, and region at the macro level—and the same infighting within the group.

Another feature in ancient India was that the kings rarely interfered in the functioning of the village or the guilds unless their own personal interests were involved. It was not that they did not want to interfere but their attention was taken up by internecine fights among various states. Therefore, in spite of various controls and systems, the grass-roots operations remained the same. For example, the administration at the village and district level rarely changed. Even during the medieval and the Mughal periods, only the nomenclatures changed while the functionaries, by and large, remained the same. During the medieval period, the guild system, barring a few breakdowns, got gradually strengthened. What was also interesting was that whenever there was any interference in the normal functioning of institutions like the guilds, there was confusion. However, when the guilds were left to themselves, they did try to evolve certain criteria of selecting the heads, rules and norms based on the prevailing social values.

Management in British India

During the British period, many companies in the United Kingdom started setting up manufacturing units in India. Initially, these mainly related to jute, textile and plantations. Later on, they moved to the exploitation of coal. Such companies were located in London and institutionalised the system of managing agencies. These agencies were located in India and managed the enterprises on behalf of the parent company. This also helped, later on, in creating a class of professional managers. Gradually, some of the enterprises were taken over by Indian entrepreneurs acting as managing agents, and, in the process, bringing in their systems, family loyalties and conflicts.

There were times when the British tried to bring improvements and impose their system. For example, separating the executive and the judiciary functions at the district/county level created problems and they reverted to centralised combined controls. This happened in the case of district administration as well as in the management of enterprises. A unique feature of the British system was that they tried to institutionalise the decision-making process by bringing in rules and regulations. They also tried to formalise the administration of justice by developing elaborate judicial machinery based on specific Indian practices.

Another feature of Indian administration was the mistrust of the people, which harked back to the ancient days and continued during the British period. This mistrust got reinforced after 1857 when there was a large-scale rebellion against British rule.

A dominant feature of Indian administration was the availability of the head whom people or employees could approach for redressal of their grievance. For example, the administrator combined in himself all the functions and was considered as *Maibaap* (mother and father) for the people of the district/county. This had both advantages and disadvantages. The advantage was that the employees could get their grievances resolved without delay. However, middlemen could misuse such a practice and also delay remedial measures.

Management in Independent India

After independence, many managers and academicians thought of professionalising management. In that context, professionalisation meant the western approach that comprises scientific management in the Taylorian way; an accent on formal systems, rules and regulations; the behavioural science approach to management of human resources, etc. Later, some concepts like management by objectives (MBO) and organisation development (OD) also became fashionable, at least on paper. Collective bargaining became an important means of regulating employer–employee relations.

The advocacy of 'modern' concepts led to further confusion, especially when they were applied suddenly to a very traditional society. Therefore, Indian management ended up with a lot of dilemmas in its actual practice. There was one set of practices, based on 'modern' concepts which existed on paper; and there was another set which employees perceived was actually being followed and which was based on traditional concepts. This resulted in dissatisfaction among employers as well as employees. The former blamed the latter for not accepting 'modern' professional management concepts, while the employees blamed the employers for ad hoc decisions and for not following the 'stated' policies.

The major cause for confusion has been the need to adapt to a different norm and practice each time a foreign concept has been imposed. This has been the bane of Indian administration and management through the ages.

Indianness Retained

Intermingling of cultures has been the history of India. This led to the constant adoption, synthesis and regeneration of administrative and management practices. Despite varying degrees of influence from outsiders upon it at various points of time, it has retained its essential Indianness.

Norms and Expectations

The broad concepts of management and administration are, in a sense, universal. The culture-specificity arises in the extent to which these are applied. The concepts of planning, recruitment, training, financial systems and control, are there in any culture. In India, too, such universal principles and concepts of management and administration existed through the ages. But there is a subtle variation in how planning is carried out; how much is completed; how recruitment takes place; how the financial controls are effected; and so on. The difference arises because Indian management and administrative practices reflect the norms and expectations of the people.

Paternalism appears to be the cornerstone of the Indian social and cultural order—and, by extension, in Indian organisations as well. Tied to paternalism are such traits as familialties, a sense of security, respect for seniority, importance of the personality of the leader, forms of authoritarianism, obedience of authority, and patronage. These operate in varying degrees in a complex matrix in the Indian environment. It is found that they are not written down as official policy, but are tacitly understood and practised.

Paternalism evokes a very favourable response in Indian organisations. Paternalism revolves around a father figure or an elder who is the guiding spirit. It is a form of general guardianship that pervades formal roles in an organisation. There is a sense of collective security about paternalism. It identifies with the larger good of the institution—the human aspect of it.

Unlike paternalism, the system of patronage is internecine and based on the principle of the individual exploiting the system to his/her own end. While not always to the detriment of the organisation, it could, in a sense, affect the motivation of the people by dividing the organisation into different camps. Consequently, it can affect cohesion within the organisation. There are, however, some strengths in the system. The subtle advantages gleaned from patronage can be a motivation in itself. While patronage is not the best thing for the organisation, it ensures a certain continuity.

Historically the genesis of the system of patronage was the king or ruler not being from among his people. An 'outsider' king needed 'his own people' to build and maintain his control over the kingdom. Further, rivalries and intrigues accentuated the move from paternalism, towards patronage. Cliques and 'followers' were spawned as a consequence and the system took root. The history of Indian administration and, by extension (though to a lesser degree), management of industry is rife with examples of such happenings.

For the Indian industry and management today, patronage is a congenital malady, which is rooted in the paternalistic mindset. Patronage thrives in situations of conflicting interest at the top. The battle lines may be drawn on bases as different as two sons of the founder-chairman in the case of the traditional family-owned company; an 'outsider' chief executive as in the public sector; caste or regional affiliations; or social and educational background. In Indian organisations, interactions, formal and informal, determine one's position in the familial structure. It is found that in all Indian organisations, MNCs and public sector, harmony is easier achieved when due deference is given to the familiality, seniority and age.

There is a sense of security that goes with this closer identification with the larger whole in organisations.

The history of industrial organisations in India could well be called personality-centred. Throughout ancient India, the rulers consolidated in themselves the power of governance and authority. The laws of the time depended much on the outlook and personality of the ruler, though there had been attempts at standardisation of power and authority based on the expectations of people over time.

In the modern day context too it seems that the personality factor is crucial in the organisational setting. It contributes a great deal to making the organisational atmosphere and climate what it is. The number of people who cite the reason for either the success or failure of planning (in any type of organisation) is itself the evidence of its predominance. The top management likes to take decisions, they say, implying that it is the repository of organisational initiative and, in effect, the organisational personality.

Organisational Plans and Policies

In 50 to 60 per cent of the organisations included in the sample study, plans or policies formulated in different areas do work as conceived, in the perception of the managers. Certain functions in these organisations, ranging from the instrument of delegation, long term and short-term goals, and manpower policy, to the financial system, technology upgradation, marketing and information systems were taken into consideration. While different reasons appear to contribute to the functioning of the plans/policies in different areas, some common reasons appear widespread in the Indian environment (see Table 1.1).

According to many Indian managers, centralised decision making, non-interference in the implementation of plans or policies, and the presence of plans that are suited to existing conditions appear to be major reasons for plans working as conceived. In particular areas there are other reasons. The instrument of delegation appears to work because there is an evolved culture of delegation and collective decision-making, in the preparation of managers, is prevalent in nearly half the organisations. According to them, easy comprehension of the plan also contributes to the working of the instrument of delegation.

In the case of technology upgradation and financial systems, the formal procedures mentioned in Table 1.1, it appears, are the major contributory factors in addition to the common ones. Staff approval of the plan appears important for the policy regarding employee participation in management. The formal procedures also contribute to the working of the plan regarding the appraisal system.

Again, in the perception of the managers, a substantial number of policies and plans do not work as conceived. Either they do not work or there are deviations in their implementation. The top management likes to take decisions without consulting others; plans are made only for records; and, to an extent, the interference of caste, community, regional affiliations, nepotism, system of patronage and external pressures lead to these deviations (see Table 1.2).

The top management, which itself encourages deviations in the plans, is mainly responsible for the failure of the plans/policies relating to instruments of delegation, and the financial and information systems. According to the managers, within the

Table 1.1 Whether the Organisational Policies have Worked and Reasons Why

Policy Areas	Instrument of Delegation	Long-term Goals	Short-term Goals	Manpower Policy	Complement of Staff/ Manning Norms	Appraisal System	Transfers	Employees Participation in Management	Financial Systems	Technological Upgradation	Materials/ Inventory Management System	Information Systems	Marketing Strategy
Planned	91.8	94.1	97.6	95.3	86.0	97.0	54.7	46.5	84.9	84.8	69.7	87.2	68.6
Worked	63.3	48.1	60.7	46.3	52.7	34.5	40.4	25.0	68.6	53.4	68.5	57.3	74.6
Reasons for plans working													
Plans suit existing conditions	40.0	41.0	66.7	57.9	41.0	51.7	36.3	70.0	46.0	48.7	43.9	27.3	70.4
Plans easily comprehended	46.0	25.6	41.2	18.4	25.0	37.9	21.1		32.0	33.3	36.5	44.1	47.7
No interference	40.0	38.5	33.3	34.2	40.0	65.5	52.6	30.0	34.0	25.6	34.1	44.1	25.0
Plan informal/flexible	22.0	28.2	33.3	13.2			26.3	40.0	12.0	12.8	34.1		36.4
Staff approves plan	16.0	13.7	13.7		31.0	31.0	21.1	50.0		66.7		15.9	
Decision making centralised	32.0	53.8	31.4	55.3	51.2	31.0	63.2	40.0			53.6	46.5	
Evolved culture of delegation	54.0								46.0				36.4
Collective decision making	54.0												
Different system of accountability		23.1	29.2	13.2	14.5			30.0	48.0		21.4	20.9	
Union co-operative		7.8	7.8	13.2									27.3
Formal procedure						62.0	42.1		64.0	48.7	43.9	39.5	25.0

All figures are in percentages. N = 86.

TABLE 1.2 Whether the Organisational Policies have not Worked and Reasons Why

Policy Areas	Instrument of Delegation	Long-term Goals	Short-term Goals	Man-power Policy	Complement of Staff/ Manning Norms	Appraisal System	Transfers	Employees Participation in Management	Financial Systems	Technological Upgradation	Material/ Inventory Management System	Information Systems	Marketing Strategy
Planned	91.8	94.1	97.6	95.3	86.0	97.0	54.7	46.5	84.9	84.8	69.7	87.2	68.6
Did not work	35.4	50.6	34.5	48.8	44.6	60.7	57.5	55.0	27.4	39.7	26.6	37.3	18.6
Reasons													
The top management likes to take decisions without consulting others	67.9	36.5	37.9	57.5	54.5	51.0	68.1	85.0	85.0	34.5	31.25	71.4	36.6
Subordinates not experienced enough	25.0												
Difficult to pin responsibility in case of failure	60.7	29.2	24.1			15.7	26.0	13.6	35.0		56.25	21.4	
Decision making in organisation centralised						15.7		45.0		31.0			63.6
Plans made only for records	71.4	51.2	58.6	55.0	45.5	64.7	59.3	68.1		31.0			
Plans not suited to existing conditions	17.9	10.0	34.5	25.0	30.3	27.4	18.5		20.0	17.2	31.25	53.5	72.7
Staff does not approve of plan				25.0	18.2	39.2	29.6		25.0	34.5			

continued

Table 1.2 continued

Policy Areas	Instrument of Delegation	Long-term Goals	Short-term Goals	Man-power Policy	Complement of Staff/Manning Norms	Appraisal System	Transfers	Employees Participation in Management	Financial Systems	Technological Upgradation	Material/Inventory Management System	Information Systems	Marketing Strategy
Formal procedure not followed	21.4	12.1	13.8		12.1	3.7	33.3		65.0		43.75	42.8	45.5
Interference of caste/ community/regional affiliation/nepotism/ system of patronage/ external pressure	14.3	56.0	44.8	67.5	63.6	72.5	74.0	22.7		58.6		14.2	
Few people understand it		9.3	10.3	25.0		7.8				13.8			
Top management encourages deviation	42.9	36.5	24.1		33.3			27.2		31.35	31.25	46.4	
People prefer it this way	14.3		10.3			7.8	14.8					17.8	
Management un-cooperative								22.7		44.8			
Union un-cooperative													
Lack of appropriate information system		14.6	13.8		39.4	7.8			40.0			21.4	
Others		7.3											

All figures are in percentages. N = 86.

instrument of delegation, a major reason for deviation is the difficulty in pinning responsibility in case of failure. This also contributes to deviations in the policy regarding the materials/inventory management system.

The managers questioned felt that un-cooperative unions affect policies regarding manpower and technology upgradation while the marketing strategies go off-track because formal procedures are not followed and plans itself are not suited to existing conditions.

Four Types of Organisations

On the face of it, there are four types of Indian organisations with enough similarities so as to club them all together. At the same time there are dissimilarities in certain areas that set them apart from each other. There is no fine line that separates certain policies or norms as typical of one type of organisation. In each there is a derived strength and, in some cases, an inherent weakness. As a composite whole, it is not as if one is qualitatively better than the other but all are patently 'Indian'.

One thing does stand out, and that is that the differences among the different types of Indian organisations are only perceived differences. These are the cumulative effect of subtle variations in the degree of importance and applicability of various factors affecting the organisation. Within the different areas of management, ranging from instruments of delegation and planning to personnel policies and finance, the concerns in all four types of organisations are similar.

Dualism in Indian Management

Management in India is characterised by a peculiar dualism. This is due to the conflict that arises from having alien systems thrust on resident practices and expectations. Professed policies and procedures are not followed within the organisation. It thus appears that, on the face of it, the entire management is not working. And yet organisations do move and, by and large, produce substantial results. This is because, as many have said, management in the organisation is effective 'somehow'. The dualism lies here.

People's expectations have a socio-cultural basis. In any organisation, the practices and norms that are followed through history have a definite place and leave a deep mark. By and large, people do expect a sense of continuity in the present practices. The expectations of people that have developed over 3,000 years do not change almost overnight, so to say.

The expectations of people in relation to management and organisations are based mainly on paternalism and its varied details. Personality and its attendant organisational manifestations are central to the Indian environment. To these, a degree of centralisation is expected. Mild authoritarianism is tolerated as is a certain amount of discretionary power in the hands of the trusted top man. A sense of belongingness and other traditional Indian idiosyncrasies are what people in Indian organisations expect.

These expectations, with the difference between organisations manifested only in a matter of degrees, it appears, have no place in the scheme of things in the essentially western management system. Any of the traditional Indian traits do not appear to be factors in the formulation of policies or procedures. These policies are drafted on the basis of foreign management principles and theories. The dualism arises when there is a gap between the stated policies and the actual practices in organisations which are based on people's expectations.

What is normally argued is that since work gets done anyway, it must be taking place according to policies and procedures. Hence the popular misconception that 'Indian management is what is laid down in policies and recorded norms'. However, this is only an illusion; what is actually happening is quite something else. The actual practices are what Indian management is all about.

There are numerous theories which hold that Indian management will benefit greatly by going back to the 'glorious days' of

Indian history. The virtues of the ancient king, Lord Rama and the wisdom of Lord Krishna expressed through the Gita (the Hindu sacred book) will, it is said, make Indian management vibrant, active and effective.

However, little consideration is given to the fact that the virtues of kings of ancient times and the effectiveness of a particular management stem from the culture and environment of the time. They are wholly irrelevant to the modern organisation.

Further, a realistic assessment of the historical context in which the ancient scriptures like the Ramayana, Mahabharata, Quran or Bible were set would reveal that the time was rife with family feuds and internecine conspiracies. The royal family, which was the focus of these turmoils, would have been the bane of any administration or government. Transporting modernisation to such an environment would be a perfect recipe for disaster.

Little thought has been given by pontiffs of the 'go-back-to-the-old' school to the fact that much water has since flowed under the bridge. The prosperity and efficiency of those times cannot be replicated by merely faithfully initiating its virtues. There is no going back and Indian management would do best to wake up to the fact that the present socio-cultural milieu is far different from what it was then.

Practices and norms in the Indian environment, in different areas under the discipline of management, differ from those followed in a foreign environment. The traits that are particularly Indian, and those common to foreign management practices (mainly western-American) are listed here. In a sense, Indian management would be the manifestation of the cumulative whole.

Future Directions

The pursuit of excellence and efficiency has brought the world of management to where it presently stands. There is a perpetual question of 'where now from here?' It has been the endeavour of every management thinker to find an answer. Such an answer has been based on the study of the present and lessons from the

TABLE 1.3 **Management Practices**

Practice	Indian	Foreign
• Instrument of delegation	— More informal instrument — Detailed laid-down instrument — Reluctance to accept responsibility — Top management encourages decisions being referred to it	— Instrument exists or there is increasing tendency to delegate — Delegation based on a greater thrust on laid-down norms
• Planning	— Long-range planning does exist but is not followed — Only short-term plans and/or profit orientation in some organisations	— Both short- and long-term plans exist — Accent on short-term planning and profits in the West; long-term in Japan
• Manpower policy	— Based on experience and expediency, resulting in surplus and shortages	— Policy based on work and method study — Open method of hire and fire at the workplace; but there is job security in Japan
• Recruitment	— Policy exists but actual practice is based on expediency — Non-organisational considerations matter but is denied	— Policy exists — Emphasis on implementation
• Training	— No planned training — No follow-up on need identification — More funds for managerial training but far less or none for worker training or skill upgradation	— Planned managerial training — High level of orientation and post-experience training
• Appraisal system	— Policy exists — Does not work — No faith in formal system — 'Selectively' used in promotion and development	— Policy exists — Plays major role in promotion and development
• Promotion	— Policy exists; based ambiguously on suitability/seniority/merit — Consequence: an unsure sense of dissatisfaction with policy — Seniority has greater weightage	— Policy exists; based on merit/appraisal — In Japan it is based on seniority and length of service

continued

Table 1.3 continued

• Transfer	— No clearly laid-down policy — Subtly subverted to be used mainly as an instrument of reward and punishment	— Transfers effected by mutual agreement in most cases
• Grievance handling	— Laid down procedures exist — Procedures largely remain unused — Often settled through unions, collective strength, system of paternalism or 'darbars' (open door system by the top management)	— Policy exists — Procedures, by and large, followed as per laid down norms
• Employees participation in management	— Policy exists — Employees go through the procedure without sincerity — Instrument of collective bargaining suppresses participation	— Little actual participation — In some countries like West Germany and Yugoslavia, specific laws exist
• Perspective on trade unions	— Looked upon varyingly as an unnecessary factor in decision-making or as a necessary legal formality — Too much political influence, and external leadership. Gradually an internal trade union leadership is emerging.	— In most cases the management and the trade unions are in adversary positions
• Approach towards employees	— Policy generally projects employees as a factor of production — Employees generally treated on the basis of paternalism or patronage	— Policy exists in that it is often divorced from closeness between employees and management — Treated as a factor of production
• Information systems	— Policies and norms laid down — Policies are not followed since procedures are not followed — Information treated as something to be shared selectively — Top management does not follow any pattern — Top management itself encourages deviation	— Specific laid-down channels — Smoother operation since systems are suited to the structure and people

continued

Table 1.3 continued

Practice	Indian	Foreign
• Financial system	— Policy exists — Top management encourages deviation by overriding policy	— Policy exists — Procedures are laid-down — Strong accent on short-term profitability; but long-term perspective and profitability taken more seriously in Japan
• Technology	— Policy and norms exist — Considerations are other than technology	— Based on policies and norms — In many cases preparatory work is done before any change
• Expansion/ diversification	— Factors influencing decision are often non-organisational — Policy not strictly followed	— Based on policy and norms — Considerations: organisational growth and need
• Marketing	— Policy exists — Not strictly followed so as to meet targets and goals — Frequent change in plans	— Policy exists — By and large followed

past. Management in India is by no means different in this respect. There has been a subtle eclipsing of the 'perpetual question' here because there has not been a systematic and effective gauge of the state of the present, nor has there been a focused exploration of management traditions in India. With the identification of the practices and traits of Indian management and the understanding of the lessons of the history of administration and management in the country, the following question craves an answer: Whither Indian management?

Undeniably the centrepiece in Indian management is the personality of the top man in the organisation. It has been so throughout history and in all likelihood will remain the same in the near future. The principal reason for this is that our policies and social structures are still built around the personalities of leaders.

Given this, it would appear that a movement towards greater efficiency in Indian management is highly dependent on the leader. However, that is not wholly so. Leaders in the organisation are themselves susceptible to numerous external pressures. For one, in the case of chief executives, their future in the job itself is dependent on the pleasure of their superiors. The insecurity and the pressures of having to produce immediate tangible results influence their approach to the organisation.

Further, in present-day Indian management there is little serious attempt at the standardisation and institutionalisation of practices, and consequently, the expectations. This is the bane of effective management. There is little continuity in crucial areas of management, especially in the public sector. The effect of fleeting personalities across the stage of leadership in the organisation compounds the confusion.

Also, people in Indian organisations appear to be subtly conditioned against the success of any outsider who is brought in as a leader. There are exceptions, but these are few and far between. Leaders from within the organisation gain an easier and a wider acceptance.

So what does this augur for Indian management in the future? One thing that does stand out is that Indian management should institutionalise and standardise practices across organisations.

As is revealed from history, Indian management has passed through turbulent periods throughout the ages. Though some of our epics, and later, some books, refer to certain periods as the 'golden age' or 'Rama Rajya', an objective assessment reveals that the lot of the common people was extremely bad. In fact, such people were used by the state and the higher-ups to settle internecine conflicts. Therefore, the references to 'Rama Rajya' and 'golden age' are mainly due to poor documentation of facts and the lack of a sense of history.

Even in the present-day context, modern concepts of management are followed to the last detail on paper. Yet the remnants of management history still dominate the thinking of several organisations. Today's organisations—caught in a system where the patronage of the man at the top, and not merit, counts in all aspects of management—should institutionalise career planning, annual appraisal of employees (mainly for development purposes), recruitment, placement, training, etc.

In this attempt at institutionalisation, the endeavour should be to overcome the weaknesses of earlier systems of management. At the same time, the strengths and virtues of those systems have to be built up as institutional norms and structures.

The virtues of India's past are internal democratisation (as in the trade and artisan guilds and panchayats), caring paternalism (as in the family) and primacy of the institution rather than individual (that was there in certain times of ancient India).

To an extent, the British did try to institutionalise specific administrative and management practices in India. These were handed down as a legacy to the new nation. Although formal and institutional practices and norms do exist now, there is a tendency to revert to the old ways. It must be accepted that an attempt at institutionalising is a long-term proposition. An immediate and hurried effort at such a process could result either in its outright rejection or in its slow phase-out. A planned and gradual movement towards institutionalisation will definitely impart a greater degree of permanence.

This does entail a focus on foresight and planning, especially where leadership succession is concerned. This will have two advantages. One, it eliminates speculation about future leadership and, two, it grooms the incumbent for the position. Speculation regarding the future of leadership within organisations leads to the system of patronage.

Patronage warps the cordiality that lubricates the interactional functioning of Indian organisations. The expectation of the people is paternalism. The essential requisite for paternalism appears to be unity in the leadership, and a single, identifiable source of power. Duality in this regard spawns patronage. The line of succession, if not clear, will lead to people lobbying for the position and, in the process, subtly divide the organisation into cliques.

The expectation being paternalism, with a well-thought-out succession plan the next leader could be groomed as to ensure a smooth running of the organisation. It does appear that for motivational levels to be high, the leader has to meet the expectations of the people, in addition to being paternalistic to them.

The employee in Indian organisations still wants to be dependent on the superiors and the organisation for personal security and organisational needs. In this context, it may be worth mentioning that the Indian employee is not so much impressed with setting his own goals or key result areas (KRAs). On the contrary, if he gets a paternalistic treatment and a feeling of security, he does not mind his goals being set by his superiors. He even goes to them and asks for their advice and guidance on his own tasks and goals.

The feeling of security in Indian organisations, apart from being a strong motivator, has certain advantages. People accept paternal authority of the leader. The system of punishment in the organisation should be an exercise of paternal authority through short-term denial of familial security.

Absorption of the culture and ways of the organisation will be an important part of the process of grooming of leaders. Identifying the future leaders early would facilitate their understanding of the behavioural expectations of them as leaders in the organisation, their upcoming role and the responsibilities that go with it. This would go a long way in building and strengthening the institution.

Further, succession planning would undoubtedly insulate the organisation from periodic upheavals that accompany changes in leadership. There will be a certain continuity in the perspectives and the practices. It will also lend a sense of stability to the organisation over a period of time. Leaders can then extend the span of their perspective for the organisation beyond their immediate tenure, and look ahead without fear of discontinuation of their plans and ventures after they leave the organisation.

What is obviously required in Indian management is a movement away from short-term profitability and towards long-term institution-building. Right now, the personality of the leader overwhelms the institution. In such cases, it will be the responsibility of the leader to build traditions and practices that are conducive to long-term institution-building and planning. It could be spread out over a period of time with a gradual institutionalising of norms and practices while shifting the accent from the personality to the organisation itself.

Till the institutionalisation of practices gains ground in India fully, the personality factor may continue to play a role for some time to come. Therefore, identification of managers at the earlier stages and then training them so that they imbibe the culture of the organisation and learn the long-term benefits of institutionalising customs would go a long way in developing certain established norms and practices of Indian management for the future.

The supervisory method based on the old paternalistic system (where age and experience are given more prominence) should be evolved to support the carefully engineered placements in the organisation. The model organisation is not one in which, as is widely believed in India today, one man runs a spectacular show while he is there, only to see it crumble after his exit. The model organisation is one which can run on its own pace by certain established norms and practices irrespective of the leader. The gradual imbibing of this notion into organisations will mark the beginning of modern Indian management. A strong system of career planning within the organisation, which addresses itself to the training of people for future executive placements, is indispensable for obliterating the clique-oriented and personality-dominated managements in various organisations.

In Indian management, there is a strong preference for an internal leader over an external one. A greater harmony in the organisation can be achieved by growing leadership within it. Internal promotions are looked upon far more favourably than the imposition or entry of outsiders. Hence the need for a systematic career planning in the organisation. This also reduces the feeling of frustration and powerlessness of the people within the organisation, as they feel assured that competence leads to prospects of internal promotion.

The need for career planning at all levels within Indian organisations is definitely felt but given little consideration. The growth of people within the organisation is often unplanned and quite haphazard. Consequently, expectations are mixed, and in many cases discontentment is high. Growth in fits and starts does upset people, telling unfavourably on their motivation. Systematic career planning coupled with proper training and development, ensures a satisfying growth for the people.

Greater emphasis should be laid on proper selection so that once people join the organisation, they remain with the organisation. It may be worthwhile identifying people when they are young, and then moulding them to the organisation's requirements. Even if organisations have to spend more for their training, it should be treated as an investment. The projection should be on the basis of long-term employment in the organisation and identifying with the organisation. At the same time, organisations need to accept the fact that employees do leave the organisation for what they perceive as better prospects.

Placement will need greater emphasis. In most western countries, placement is considered a managerial prerogative. However, in India, it may have to be linked with the strengths of the individual rather than a 'lawful order of the superior'. While placements are worked out more as ad hoc measures and on the basis of convenience, it should be recognised that placements should be worked out on the basis of individual capabilities. It should be planned well in advance and in keeping with projected individual growth and career planning.

Another crucial point in regard to growth is the strong belief in seniority. It does not go down well with the purists who insist that merit alone should prevail. The perpetuation of the conflict arises from the lack of any planned growth or development. The point is, if seniority is crucial in motivational well-being, the attempt should be made to ensure that the senior-most is also the most meritorious. This principle would stand Indian management in good stead, if only a serious look is given into the way training and development are carried out.

The seniority principle has its own advantages as one can plan in advance what position an employee is likely to be placed in the years ahead. Since seniority and other non-merit factors will have some weightage in promotions, the annual appraisal system should be used to identify the strengths and weaknesses of employees for their future development than exclusively for promotion purposes.

It is also imperative that in any annual appraisal, the accent should not only be on weaknesses but also on strengths. It is much easier to develop people in their areas of strength rather than in areas of weakness. Therefore, any appraisal system must concentrate more on identifying the strengths of the individual in the context of organisational needs. These strengths then have to be matched with the placement of the individual.

Another point that Indian management studiously ignores is the training and development of the non-managerial or workers cadre. Very little investment goes into this when compared to the size of outlay for managerial training. Skill upgradation, something given so much importance in countries like Japan and Korea, carries little weight in India. As a result, not only do the skill levels of the workers remain low, but competence and motivation are also adversely affected. Suspicion and conflicts between the workers and the management also arise as a result. Added to this is the fact that the level of the worker's commitment to the betterment of the organisation is also low.

In any case of technology transfer, the normal tendency is to plan on the basis of manning standards originally given by the manufacturers—generally from western countries. However, in Indian organisations, any such 'speed-feed' technology transfer and manning standards result in problems due to different norms, cultural values and socio-economic conditions. As a result, all manning norms get distorted as no Indian yardsticks have been developed. Moreover, in India, there is no wholesale transfer of technology. In most cases, there is a blending of indigenous and imported technology. Therefore, in Indian conditions, it may be worthwhile to make a detailed study of the various factors which influence manning standards so that different yardsticks and norms which are more suited to Indian conditions are developed.

The same goes for productivity yardsticks as well. There is a tendency to compare productivity on the basis of western standards of productivity per man-hour. But the actual working conditions in the West or Japan are totally different from those in India. Most western countries, for example, operate on a more or less full-employment basis. But in India, the levels of skills, technical competence as well as wages are very low. Besides, there are different values and traditions which affect the labour attitude, absenteeism, overtime, etc. In such a situation, even norms of measuring productivity may have to be based on investment per person or production per unit of capital employed.

As time goes by, with increasing awareness of their rights and privileges, the workers are beginning to assert themselves more. Indian management cannot ignore the fact that the workers' participation will be the norm in the future. The sooner they awaken to this realisation, and voluntarily stride towards it, the more comfortable things are likely to be. Historically, there is enough evidence to indicate that whenever organisations or institutions were left on their own, they did develop an institutionalised system of participative structures based on consultation, strong social norms and consensus.

The best course in this direction would be to institutionalise the instruments of participation mixed with paternalism, as discussed earlier, over a period of time, with sincerity.

What is needed to safeguard against these inherent hazards in the Indian family system spilling over into the management of Indian organisations is to divorce the ownership of organisations from the management. As has so effectively been done in Japan, the ownership may change, but the continuity of management is maintained. This may be effected by the shareholding system not bearing any influence on the internal functioning of the organisation. It would do well for Indian management to institutionalise this approach within its structure. This could partly be achieved through modification of the laws relating to Indian companies and enterprises. The family-owned Eicher industrial group in India has set an example by handing over the management of the group to professional managers.

Similarly, in the government and the public sector too, efforts should be made towards having longer tenures for the top management with internal promotions and appropriate career and succession planning. There is a need to develop an institutionalised mechanism of bringing about changes in the organisational policies so that the policies are not based on the whims of individual personalities but there are certain checks and balances built into the institutional structure. So even if there are changes at the top, the organisations continue to function on the basis of long-term objectives.

What it all finally boils down to is that Indian management is resilient and can withstand the infusion of practices and principles alien to it. But the important thing is that any foreign norm should be adapted to Indian conditions. There are strong currents of expectations of the people. Foreign systems of management have to adapt to the duality of having something laid down as policies and principles while the actual practices are quite different; lest the dualism flare up into conflict and the compromises in policies and principles fail to work, it would be far better for Indian management to accept adaptive transition than risk convulsive change.

Conclusion

Management in India, then, is a complex matrix of various phenomena. It is clear that there is no separating the socio-cultural dynamics of the Indian family system and environment from the organisation. Its influence on organisational practices is very strong. Going purely by the dictates of alien management principles, however efficient they may be projected as, without allowing for the influence of 'Indianness' will mean adding to an already existing state of confusion in Indian management.

Indian management should move towards institutionalisation and standardisation of practices across organisations. This has to be done over a long term. Any attempt to hasten the process will result in its outright rejection or gradual phasing out.

Indian management needs to move away from short-term profitability and towards long-term institution-building. If, as it is at present, the personality of the leader overwhelms the institution, it should be his responsibility to build traditions and practices that are conducive to long-term institution-building.

Little attention is paid to career planning. This will only lead to discontent. Organisations must have systematic career planning for employees from the time they join.

Indian management can absorb principles alien to it. But these principles should be modified to suit Indian conditions.

Notes and References

1. **Virmani, B.R.** and **Rao, Kala,** *Economic Restructuring, Technology Transfer and Human Resource Development,* Response Books, Sage Publications, New Delhi, 1997, pp. 43–44.
2. **Virmani, B.R.** and **Guptan, Sunil Unny,** *Indian Management,* Vision Books, New Delhi, 1991.
3. The *varna* or the caste system in ancient India was based on occupational structures and not necessarily on birth.

2

Planning for Human Resource Development

One of the challenges presently before us is to harness the technology revolution for general welfare. To most of us, 'technology' conjures up images of sleek machines and computer-controlled systems. These machines, no doubt, are products and tools of the technological age but the real engine of a technology remains the human mind. The challenge to the planners, educators and those concerned with HRD is to develop the skills of workforce so that they can fully utilise the machine power that lies at our fingertips.

Unfortunately, the training tools and institutions which we have developed over the past century have often not kept pace with the geometric advances in technology. This is more true in the case of the developing countries. Our formal training institutions are, through no fault of their own, under-financed and often impart the skills of an outdated technology. In many cases, the teachers themselves are unfamiliar with the latest technology. The organisations which need this skilled manpower for their advancing processes, often have to choose between the options available based on obsolete techniques. This further inhibits the introduction of new technology because skilled operators are not available. There could also be instances where the teachers who are good at imparting skills and the organisations which know what needs to be taught, often have no effective means of communication. Therefore, for any technology changes and development, there is need for both short-term and long-term planning for human resources. Thus, technological planning as well as human resource planning must go hand in hand.

Planning Process for HRD

The objective of the planning activity is to establish the framework for evaluation and the evaluation process should then feed the next stage of the planning process. Developing people is the centre of the planning circle. Planning leads to setting of objectives (specific, measurable, outcome-oriented statements) which, in essence, become the lynchpins of the planning, administration and evaluation functions. It is easy to theoretically develop the planning and evaluation process but very difficult to carry it out in a very complex, technologically-mobile environment, as there are many points at which it can break down. Before we start the actual planning process, some of the major questions to be answered are:

1. To what extent is the planning process routinely tied to specific data?
2. Do we have sufficient data on the basis of which to make HRD programme decisions?
3. Do we have an HRD Management Information System (MIS)?
4. To what extent are the plans evaluated and used in the next planning cycle?
5. Is the plan or the outcomes reviewed at the end of the plan period? Is the data from the evaluation of the current plan recycled into the next plan?

The planning should be specific enough so that an HRD plan can be developed which will determine where a country or an organisation can best obtain or train the human resources needed to accomplish the specific objectives. In such cases, the objectives have to be clear and possibly measurable and the HRD plan is related to visibly assisting the country's programmes keeping in view the changes taking place in technology and environment.

HRD is normally relegated to the sidelines when technological and developmental planning is done. But there are several things that can be taken up by HRD planners in the course of the technological development:

1. Develop an HR plan. Even if there are no specific country-level developmental objectives or if the plans are so generic that they do not permit HRD plans to be effectively linked to it, one can still think in terms of some such plan. While the plan will get linked to different elements and will not be focused on specific outcomes, it can still be carried out. On the contrary, the HRD development plan can, in certain cases, set an example for the national planners.
2. Effectively integrate the development of specific plans regarding the new technologies.
3. Ask planning-related questions, for example, how many and of what types of personnel and what skills will the country need in various sectors of the economy over the next five to 10 years? What new knowledge and skills will the country need over the next few years to facilitate technological development?
4. What major problems do the planners feel must be overcome in the near future to meet the objectives (all these may not be subject to HRD solutions; but some are)? Some initial steps could be:
   (a) Long-range and short-range components are needed. Given the planning requirements, we should look to the future, but how far ahead depends on many factors. Many experts feel that 15–20 year plans may be irrelevant because of rapid technological changes which are difficult to predict. The most common long-range planning period in many countries is five years.

(b) Each segment of the economy must be linked to the overall country's goals. Therefore, each segment including its HRD wing should base its plans on the national plans.

(c) Provisions for the review and modification of the plan are necessary. There has to be an annual review of the long-range plan to take care of the environmental and technological changes.

It is important that the HRD and technological plans are linked with the budgetary allocations. Each HRD segment should have a planning timetable that provides for completing the plan before the budget is 'locked in'. This will ensure that the plan is realistic and that the resources needed to fund the plan are appropriate and available. This will require that the planning be data-based.

Education and Training

In any planning process for technological changes, the basic pre-requisite is education, especially higher education. In many countries (India is one example) one of the reasons for the expansion of higher education is the planners' main concern with forecasting and meeting the needs of higher level manpower and their tendency to err on the side of excess supply. The demand for higher-level professional manpower has been determined on the assumptions of fixed output-skill ratios. The possibilities of substituting between physical capital and skills and among different skill categories have been ignored. This leads to rigidities in the system. Investments in education tend to be made without any reference to socio-economic criteria. Educational institutions are thus established without regard to the availability of material as well as human resources, adequacy of catchment areas, optimal size and socio-economic needs. In such a situation, there is more emphasis on expansion rather than on improving the quality and efficiency of the existing resources. Some of the indicators of the malfunctioning of educational systems in countries of the Indian subcontinent are:

(a) High rate of unemployment among the educated;
(b) scarcity of certain skills;
(c) high level of brain-drain;
(d) under utilisation of employed skills; and
(e) high rate of failures and drop-outs.

There is wastage of resources at all levels of the educational system, primarily at the school level. For example, in India, there is a very high drop-out rate, almost 50 per cent, in the first four years of school. It is very high compared to Japan (1 per cent); Taiwan (8 per cent); South Korea (less than 10 per cent); Afghanistan (15 per cent) and the Philippines (about 20 per cent).[1] Even in the engineering colleges, the drop-out rate in India is fairly high and there is unemployment among the engineers. It has been estimated that the investment made on one drop-out from an engineering college can take care of at least one primary school for a year.

The Indian subcontinent has a large number of scientists and engineers but because of the lack of a systematic approach to link theoretical training with the socio-economic environment, the technological development of the society has been slow. In these countries, technology has been imported even for simple industrial processes. This can lead to failure of educational policies on the criteria of investment, redistribution and creation of socially relevant needs. Consequently, this can lead to inefficiencies in the production as well as the utilisation of human capital.

Another factor is that academic training distinctly designed for HRD is not widespread in universities and colleges. It should be understood that HRD presumes not merely development of literacy or education but developing people for the required skills with specific objectives. Therefore, educational institutions need to develop a distinct HRD focus. This is not to indicate that investment in school education is irrelevant as it provides the basic material for higher technical education. If the basic material is poor, then investments in higher technical education may not yield the desired results.

With a view to modernising the conventional production system, machinery and technical know-how are initially imported from the advanced countries either in exchange of primary goods or as external assistance to be repatriated later. But these practices cannot go on forever. Therefore, some countries have started laying emphasis on developing their own technical personnel to operate complicated technological systems. Therefore, more investments will be needed in higher education, which will stress the development of skills for new technologies.

For appropriate skill development, many countries have started vocational training institutes as well as apprenticeship training schemes. However, the quality of training schemes is deficient in two senses. One, the trainee is unable to do a specific job although he/she is regarded as capable of doing it. Two, the training fails to reach a certain standard. In this case, a vague relationship between training and the ability to do a specific job is being established and the emphasis is upon the development of the trainees' talents for a broad range of jobs. Here, the concept of training slides into that of education.

Thus, it is conceivable that the product of a 'bad' training in the second sense, can be a perfectly good worker as far as the employer is concerned. Similarly, good training in that sense can produce, from the employers' point of view, a 'bad' worker. Therefore, there is a strong movement to improve the quality of training. One reason for such a demand is the 'micro chip' revolution. A second reason can also be responsible for increasing unemployment. There is an expectation that youth must get a placement immediately after leaving school. Thus, there is more concern about training for the unemployed than training for the employed or about to be employed. In countries like France and West Germany, 40 to 50 per cent of young people enter full-time vocational education after compulsory schooling; in countries like India, it is less than 5 per cent.

Similarly, the apprenticeship training in industry is normally treated as a cheap substitute for permanent employees. The training given is of a very general nature. The objective of these schemes is normally to increase the competitive edge of the young people and get them as quickly as possible into a job. The programme is constrained by these objectives and the quality would necessarily suffer. Many of the jobs available to young people require no skill or training. For a need-based training, the starting point must be that there are jobs for which the training is required. The need, therefore, is for high-quality training for high-quality jobs.

It is understood that any investment in HRD in certain cases would yield results in the long run. The advantage is that the skills do not depreciate or lose their value during the period of their utilisation. On the contrary, the more that knowledge, skill and experience are made use of, the more is the capital value and the higher the income-yielding capacity of the investment. In fact, there is a close relationship between the spread of scientific, technical education and the pace of technological advancement, scientific inventions and innovations, and between the trained manpower and the utilisation of the advanced techniques of production, as for example, the outturn of civil engineers and the volume and value of construction activity.[2]

Changes in Occupational Structures

A number of recent studies on the relationship between new technologies and skills have reached quite different conclusions. Some feel that there is a definite trend towards de-skilling. In the printing sector, for instance, photocomposition and facsimile satellite transmission can render much of the traditional know-how of the profession obsolete. The same is true of the metal trade. Highly skilled milling, grinding and lathe machines are being replaced by computerised numerically controlled (CNC) machine tools. Another point made is that the introduction of robots would lead to general decline in qualifications because these machines take over not only the manual but also the intelligent human functions.

Others, however, do not agree with these views and argue that the production, setting-up and monitoring of these machines require vast and sophisticated know-how and skills. Yet others foresee a different polarisation of skills: those that, on the one hand, require an elite of engineers-technocrats, controllers, repairers, and, on the other, a large army of machine-minders.

Such a variety of functions may not be surprising. In the first place, new technologies are just beginning to be introduced and the occupational changes they entail are still quite unclear.[3] Moreover, microelectronics is applied in many different production processes and can, therefore, lead to very different skill patterns. It is quite possible to foresee that occupational activities will be less concerned with production processes than with control and support activities. Manual activities and craftsmanship will probably be transferred to maintenance and repair tasks that will become more complex as the machines become more sophisticated. A very high degree of occupational skills will need to be combined with higher levels of general and technical education. Therefore, the quality of education will be very important for the worker has to understand the whys and the wherefores of the limited operation for which he is responsible so that he can absorb the continuous training and retraining which technical changes are sure to entail.

Moreover, at least in certain occupations, information technology is playing an increasing role in areas from which it was totally absent only a few years ago. Figure 2.1 illustrates this in relation to electro-technical occupations. Given these trends, a broad basic education which gives a solid grounding in science will be a valuable asset for future members of the workforce which will be called upon to work with the new technologies.[4]

Another trend that is visible is the growing mass of employment in the services sector. According to a study of OECD countries, the share of employment of the services sector rose on an average from 43 per cent in 1960 to 63 per cent in 1981.[5] It now accounts for two-thirds of the total employment in the U.S. and Canada, though far less than 50 per cent in the countries of southern Europe and Ireland. It grew at a faster annual rate between 1973 and 1990 than between 1960 and 1973. This is mainly in trade, restaurants, hotels, transport and communications, public health, insurance, postal services, education and other business services. There is an increasing use of modern technologies in these services which can result in temporary displacement,

FIGURE 2.1 **Qualitative Changes in Electro-technical Occupations**

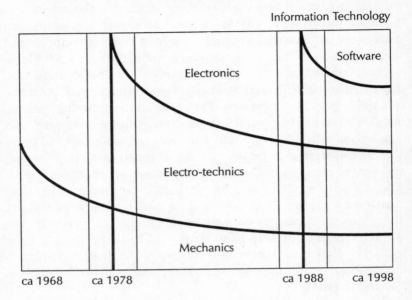

necessitating training and retraining of personnel. Therefore, specialised training programmes will have to be designed for the services sector.

In the planning process for HRD, it is necessary to analyse and examine the demand–supply relationship on a continuing basis and check the 'rolling forecasts' periodically so that suitable adjustments can be made in the determination of priorities. The long-term forecasts should go far beyond a statistical analysis giving a qualitative as well as quantitative evaluation and appraisal of changing demand–supply relationships.

While forecasting future manpower shortages, one should take into account the changes in occupational skills that are likely to take place in future. For example, a new technology will lead to the development of new skills, rendering the old skills redundant. The introduction of CNC machines in the metal trade is one example. This, at times, can create a dilemma for the economy, because in many cases, the organisations may just go in for recruitment of new persons, easing out the old ones. Thus, the HRD strategy should provide for the upgrading of the skills of the existing manpower as well as training of the new personnel. This has to be linked to the basic educational requirements and standards, right at the selection stage.

Case of an Electrical Engineering Company

As an illustration, we have analysed the data of one large heavy electrical engineering company which has upgraded its technology and introduced CNC machines.[6] With the introduction of this new technology, there is a reduction in standard man-hours which means that the labour intensity of the new production process is less than that of the earlier process. Also, the new technology results in cost and material savings, raises the productivity levels and, at the same time, ensures greater scientific precision of the final product. Let us examine the implications of the introduction of such new technology on manpower planning and HRD.

One of the tasks of human resource planners is to develop some yardsticks of manning norms in the context of technological changes. Manning standard is a subject matter of manpower planning which deals with the estimation of the demand for, and the supply of, manpower and finding the equilibrium between the two. At the micro level also, the job of the manpower planner in any organisational set-up is to estimate the various requirements of technical and non-technical manpower and its availability. Whenever there is a shift in the production process, some technological improvement, reorientation of the production methods or introduction of new machinery, the manpower department will face the problem of how best to utilise the given supply of manpower efficiently and economically.

However, the problem before the organisation is that the specifications given by the manufacturers of new machines on technical and manning standards cannot always be followed due to various reasons. First, the new machine works in a new environment surrounded by new work norms and culture. Second, the company is importing the machinery according to its specific needs, and not a complete set of a plant. Third, it cannot strictly follow the technical specifications of manning standards due to non-familiarity with the particular machine. Fourth, the management has to take into consideration the existing industrial relations situation.

Whenever some new machinery arrives, the existing jobs get disturbed, and the problem of shifting of jobs arises. For example, the introduction of CNC machines reduced the drudgery of work in general, but more importantly, reduced the content of unskilled labour. Now, the job-skills are shifting more towards planning, process planning and tooling. Two important implications, as far as manning standards are concerned, are seen. First, the nature of the existing jobs is changing from unskilled to skilled and highly-skilled levels, and second, standard man-hours are getting reduced, in turn reducing the unskilled workforce. In such a situation, keeping in view the industrial relations problem, the management is trying to 'enrich' the job and provide alternative jobs to surplus labour. Job enrichment here means that the 'worker operating such sophisticated machines has to read the charts and other instructions and should be able to coordinate his work more than he was earlier. This does not mean that the managerial part of the engineer's work has shifted to the worker. His physical drudgery is reduced but the mental alertness is increased. He is now supposed to monitor the functioning of the machine rather than involving himself physically in its operation. The impact of transfer of technology on manning standards is presented in Table 2.1. The table reveals the following important points:

1. Taking 1986–87 as the cut-off year, the gross block (fixed capital) increased from 100 per cent in 1986–87 to 399 per cent in 1995–96 while the number of workers decreased from 5,056 to 4,665 during the same period. At the same time, the total manpower has increased from 5,211 in 1986–87 to 7,035 in 1995–96, the additions taking place mostly at the supervisory and executive cadres due to changes in the nature of technology and jobs. Even if we add both the categories of employees, the growth of gross block

TABLE 2.1 **Index of Fixed Capital and Workforce in a Heavy Electrical Engineering Company in India**

Year	Gross Block (Fixed Capital) in Rs '000s	No. of Workers	Total Manpower	Index of (2)	Index of (3)
(1)	(2)	(3)	(4)	(5)	(6)
1986–87	1,33,486	5,056	5,211	100	100
1987–88	1,59,885	5,076	5,307	120	100
1988–89	1,82,934	5,816	6,043	137	115
1989–90	2,07,194	4,891	5,168	155	97
1990–91	2,44,303	6,147	6,478	183	123
1991–92	2,90,903	6,287	6,786	218	124
1992–93	3,42,754	5,823	6,874	257	115
1993–94	3,92,901	5,429	7,031	294	107
1994–95	4,61,398	5,176	7,087	346	102
1995–96	5,32,269	4,665	7,035	399	92

between 1986–87 and 1995–96 has been around 300 per cent, whereas the total manpower has increased only by 35 per cent during the same period. The shifting of skills from workers to supervisory levels in itself has raised various problems: there will be retrenchment in certain cadres while new recruitment takes place in certain other categories leading to industrial relations problems. This organisation had to face such problems for a long time.

2. As already mentioned, in any technology transfer, the displacement at the lower levels is disproportionately larger than the additions that are taking place at the higher levels. This raises the issues of appropriateness of transfer of such technology to developing countries unless there is corresponding expansion of the organisation so that the employment potential also increases or the government takes upon itself the responsibility of retraining and increasing the skills of the existing labour, which is not happening. Often, organisations are forced to arrive at settlements with the result that there is a constant complaint about surplus labour in certain categories. The resort to periodical 'voluntary' or 'forced' retirement schemes thus adds further to the total unemployment situation in the country.

In any case of technology transfer, especially from developed to developing countries, the normal tendency is to plan on the basis of manning standards originally given by the developed countries. However, in developing countries, such 'speed-feed' technology transfer and manning standards result in problems due to different norms, values and socio-economic conditions as well as the education and skill levels of the employees. As a result, all manning standards get distorted as these yardsticks were drawn up by developed countries in a particular context. Therefore, some research may be needed to identify the various factors that influence manning standards in cases of technology upgradation. Case studies of a few organisations can be prepared to see what were the originally specified standards and what actually has happened over a period of time and what are its implications for the organisation, productivity and HRD. Maybe the manning norms would be different at the initial stage, but with skill upgradation and training, these norms can gradually change. It is important to make such estimates.

Strategy of Developing Human Resources for Employment

One of the objectives of any country, specially a developing country, is to ensure full production and employment for all who are available and seek work. Therefore, the HRD strategy must be linked to the investment, the fiscal, the monetary and even the wage and price policies. The policy objectives of the HRD strategy should be to develop economically sound production-oriented employment rather than relief-oriented employment. In other words, it should stimulate and not impede the process of economic development. Therefore, a well-designed employment promotion policy should lay down in quantitative terms the employment and training targets for different sectors of the economy and also the measures necessary to realise these objectives. It is essential that such a policy be carried out within the overall framework of national development plans. Experience shows that only those countries, specially in the Asian region, which were able to achieve a compounded rate of GDP growth of 8 per cent or more succeeded in securing a progressive decline in the rate of unemployment.[7]

It would be useful to work out a detailed inventory of the technology alternatives available for each industry, and, within each industry, for each of the major processes for the guidance of the planners and policy-makers.

The general approach of the HRD strategist should take into account the following factors:

1. Identification of the areas of economic activity which are seriously handicapped due to shortages of technical, professional and skilled manpower;
2. Initiating the necessary measures for the development and training of strategic manpower; and
3. Initiating the appropriate policies for efficient utilisation of the available human resources in the country.

Manpower shortages can be broadly grouped under the following categories:

1. *Current Availability of Positions*   These are the positions for which suitable manpower of the required skills and knowledge level is not available. In the present-day context, for example, there will be shortages of computer programmers; experts in computer-aided design (CAD); and computer-aided management (CAM) positions. There could even be shortage of some skilled workers like machinists; electronic, electrical and metallurgical engineers and supervisors at the supervisory and technical levels; and of trained craft teachers and instructors in certain areas at the professional level. There could also be shortages at the top management level where persons are expected to possess a high level of technical and managerial competence in their field of specialisation. These shortages can be identified by enquiries from major establishments, which employ greater part of the skilled workers. The other method of finding these shortages is through the registration of certain vacancies with employment services.

2. *Partially Filled Positions*   Partially filled positions constitute a concealed portion of manpower shortages. Where it is difficult to locate manpower with the requisite skills, organisations lower the education and vocational training requirements or, at times, upgrade existing employees though they lack the skills. The problem of identifying partially filled positions is one of judging cases where an increase in skills would lead to significant increase in the production or in the improvement of the quality of services. In these cases, one approach could be the development of certain standards for satisfactory performance of an occupation. The standard has to be linked to the training. The type of training already given to those employees in such occupations could be examined, and where the training falls short of the required standard could be taken as an indication of partially filled positions. This can also be done through an assessment of the proportion of manpower employed in an occupation whose inadequate performance is resulting in loss of production or rendering poor quality services. This could be done on the basis of the opinion of the employers, and even trade unions, and trade testing.

3. *Manpower Requirements Linked with Shortages of Key Inputs* In certain situations, the organisations are not working to their full capacities due to certain infrastructure bottlenecks (power, raw material, spare parts, transportation, etc.). In many developing countries, especially in Asia, there is considerable underutilisation of capacity in various sectors like power, irrigation, transportation and manufacturing. The fuller utilisation of installed capacity will create additional demand for scientific, technical and skilled manpower in the country in due course.

4. *Replacement of Foreign Technical Experts*   In the initial stages of technology development, many countries take the help of the expertise of the developed countries but, in due course, each country has to train its own personnel replacing these foreign experts who have highly specialised and critical skills.

5. *Manpower Shortages due to Employment Abroad*   In some countries like India, Pakistan and Bangladesh, there is an exodus of

certain skilled categories of employees to other countries, particularly to the Middle East. At the transitory phase, such drain is unavoidable. Therefore, the country has to prepare adequate manpower at various levels to take care of such eventualities.

Role of Different Types of Training Strategies for HRD

An attempt has been made in the preceding part of this chapter to highlight some of the basic considerations that should weigh with the planners and policy-makers concerned with technological and human resource development. This part of the chapter deals with different types of HRD programmes.

1. *Institutional Training*   The organisation of technical and vocational training could be at the professional, the technical, the artisan, the craftsman and the skilled workers level. At the professional level, the training could be at the graduate level in various fields of specialisation. At the technician level, the institutional training facilities should cover the intermediate group that falls in between professionals and the skilled workers. At the artisan, craftsman and skilled worker level, there could be special vocational training programmes.

2. *Vocational Training*   The selection of vocational training programmes most appropriate to the specific needs of the country should involve consideration of the following points:

(a) *Flexibility*   Vocational training programmes at the level of craftsmen and the production process workers must have flexibility to allow inter-occupational changes within the broad range of similar occupations as the rapid pace of technological change often renders some occupations either obsolete or less important.

(b) *Adaptability*   Technological upgradation demands considerable adaptability on the part of the skilled workers so that they adjust to new processes, new machines, new raw material and methods of handling them and new forms of control devices and occupational safety measures. Vocational training should facilitate the acquisition of new skills and application of these skills to the production processes.

(c) *Economy*   The results obtained from training should be commensurate with the resources spent. This involves balancing of costs and the benefits that may accrue from training. In such a situation, the training of employed manpower may be preferred to fresh recruitment for reasons of immediate utility and shorter gestation periods.

(d) *Accessibility*   Vocational training facilities should be located in a manner that they are easily accessible to large sectors of prospective trainees as well as to industrial centres where even practical training can be organised without much difficulty and cost. This will also involve greater collaboration between educational institutions and the industry.

3. *Apprenticeship Training*   Apprenticeship training is a system wherein an employer undertakes to employ a young person and to train him/her for a specified period. The existing apprenticeship training facilities in many of the countries in the Asian region are not adequate and suffer from some defects and limitations. There could be a shortage of adequately trained instructors in the theoretical and technical subjects. There is also a great deal of confusion regarding the importance of apprenticeship schemes and the methods by which they should be established and conducted. In one study on the graduate engineer trainees conducted earlier in India by the author,[8] it was found that there is no set syllabus for the apprenticeship scheme nor a methodical and balanced programme of theoretical and practical instruction. Supervision was often lacking and, in most cases, the apprentices were used as cheap labour. This calls for the development of a national apprenticeship programme on sound and systematic lines to determine the apprenticeship trades, fix minimum standards of training, establish methods of examination and to determine the number of apprentices and skilled workers needed for each trade and occupation. The Government of India has set up an Apprenticeship

Board to bring in better standards and uniformity in apprenticeship legislation laying down the rights and objectives of employers and apprentices and prescribing rules governing the organisation and supervision of training.

Apprenticeship training as well as the training given in institutions should be 'dovetailed' in such a manner that students can develop a broad-based knowledge of their specialised engineering functions including the changes in technology and production methods which can be expected to occur in their working lives. The apprenticeship training in industry should supplement their knowledge with specialised knowledge and skills which is required for performing particular kind of jobs in an organisation. At the micro level, there should be a long-range training plan. Each organisation must be encouraged to prepare an annual and a three- or five-year plan of plant-based education and training. The basic aim should be to meet the needs of technicians and the engineers for knowledge and skills and pave the way for foreseeable changes in the occupational and skill structure of the enterprise so that they are better prepared to contribute to technological changes in future.

Another aspect linked to training is the task of selecting technicians and engineers who are capable of upgrading their education or skill levels in accordance not only with the needs of the enterprise but also their aptitude. The proper utilisation and placement of engineers after training is another aspect requiring attention.

4. *On-the-job Training*   On-the-job training which a person receives while engaged in production work, paid or unpaid, covers both in-service and pre-service training. Normally, such training combines theoretical as well as practical experience under the guidance of experts, and is determined by the needs and requirements of each organisation.

5. *Upgrading Training*   This is training for those who are already employed by providing them prospects of improving their knowledge and proficiency. In many developing countries, a large

number of workers have no opportunity to undergo formal basic training in the trades in which they are now engaged. The upgrading training assumes special significance for such persons. Supplementary courses must be available for all workers who wish to improve their general, technical or even commercial knowledge in order to facilitate their growth within the organisation. Such training could be provided within the plant itself or in training institutions through evening classes. Outside institutional and centralised training systems may be more useful for smaller establishments. In Japan, for example, there is a 'company school system' in which certain establishments have upgraded training courses for their own employees and employees of other smaller establishments which are not equipped to have their own courses.

6. *Accelerated Training*   In certain trades and occupations, where there are serious shortages of qualified personnel, there will be need for quick training for such persons. This could be more useful to meet the urgent needs of developing countries, especially for semi-skilled workers and workers not requiring highly specialised training. Such training is possible when the trainees have the necessary basic educational background and some work experience. The instructor must be a skilled craftsman with teaching ability. In such training, there has to be a close co-operation between the industry and the centres of accelerated training. The training centres must be equipped with adequate shop-floor facilities, teaching and training materials.

In addition, there will be need to provide incentives and facilities to the employees so that they can update their knowledge. These can be:

(a) Incentives for those who take up short-term or long-term courses while they are working but outside the organisation;
(b) Allowing participation in short, off-the-job training courses; and if necessary
(c) Wage and promotion policies should be designed to provide an incentive to training, leading to a situation where employees develop the motivation for continuing education without becoming obsolete too early in their careers.

7. *Training for the Traditional and Non-formal Sector* A large number of artisans, craftsmen and production workers in some countries of the Asian region are trained by their family members or acquire the skills by working under the guidance of an experienced artisan/craftsman/skilled worker. Such trainees do not pass any tests and, though they have acquired technical competence, they are inadequately trained in modern processes. The present employment trends in these countries suggest that a sizeable proportion of the available semi-skilled workers will continue to be met by traditionally trained artisans and craftsmen. Also, there is an informal sector that comprises self-employed personnel or those working in very small establishments but meets a large segment of the market demand. Many developing countries believed that economic development would sooner or later see the emergence of a modern sector (technology-wise) sufficiently large to absorb additions to the labour force and, in the process, bring about full employment. Informal activities would then disappear and those engaged in these would be absorbed into the formal sector. However, the formal sector may not be capable of generating jobs as fast as it can generate output and many developing countries have begun to realise that these informal activities will remain. Considering this situation, it may be necessary to organise training courses even for the so-called 'way side' semi-skilled or skilled workers. Very little attention has been paid to this sector except possibly in handicrafts because of its contribution to foreign exchange earnings.

8. *Training of Instructors* The quality and efficacy of training, whether in-house or outside, depend to a large extent on the knowledge and qualifications of the instructors. One often hears complaints that new institutions have been established without adequate supply of trained teachers. The problem is also to upgrade the knowledge and skill of the instructors in keeping with the changes in the technology. There is, therefore, an urgent need to constantly train the instructors with appropriate technical skills and teaching abilities.

9. *Supervisory Training* The need for supervisory training is much greater in developing countries because of the large number of workers who lack basic training and who have very limited knowledge about new techniques or job relations, job instruction and job methods. The training within industry (TWI) programmes now in operation in a large number of countries can be further extended in both scope and coverage and the quality of training improved upon.

10. *Management Development* Development of the management should form the core of any programme for HRD. It is the management that plans, coordinates, supervises and controls the processes in industries and it is a good management which ultimately ensures the effective utilisation of all available resources. Hence, top priority needs to be given to management development programmes in HRD planning. With the changes in technology, especially the advent of computers, etc., managers have to be trained in modern technology so that they can further motivate the workers to adapt to the new systems.

Training Methodologies for HRD

Until now, training was confined to schools, vocational training institutions and colleges but in future because of fast-changing technologies, non-conventional methods of training will have to be adopted. This is more relevant where mass-scale training of all sectors of the economy is necessary. There may be need to make use of television, satellite communication, telematics, etc., as methods of training. Already, there is a growing trend towards open universities in many developing countries. In India, there is a National Open University as well as regional open universities. Television and satellite communication are extensively used for training and development. These will have to be supplemented with programmed learning, development of certain lessons through correspondence and even appropriate examination and testing systems.

Computer Assisted Instruction

Computer assisted instruction (CAI) is a relatively new technique that is being used in several educational and training situations. In its simplest form, it is a computer-based interactive medium of learning using audio-visual devices.

The computer lends itself to a variety of instructional modes. Tutorial and 'drill and practice' applications emerge most frequently as viable ways of CAI training for industry and business. When using the tutorial mode of CAI, the bulk of the learning material is presented through the computer's display unit. A one-to-one, individualised relationship is established between the computer and the trainee with the computer explaining the concepts and procedures. It displays the information and asks questions and travels to the next level of instruction only when the trainee's response indicates his readiness to proceed.[9]

The features of CAI provide several potential advantages:

1. *Individualised Instruction* The trainee learns at his/her own rate of progress. The computer responds to the specific needs of the trainee.
2. *Immediate Feedback* The amount of time required to master a lesson is often cut down up to 50 per cent via CAI.[10]
3. *Novel Method* The trainees enjoy the learning process more than the conventional method as the computer has an element of novelty and appeals to a wide variety of age groups and applications.
4. *Improved Decision-making* The trainee's decision-making skills are often strengthened. The computer presents alternatives. The trainees can make a wrong decision without serious consequences and can learn how to evaluate choices in the process.[11]

The major drawback of the CAI is the initial cost. However, in the long run, the advantages of CAI far outweigh its disadvantages.

Community-based Training

It is also found that training tools and institutions, which were developed over the past century, have not kept pace with the advances of technology even in developed countries. In such a situation, it is desirable to establish community-based technical education colleges within local communities. It is hoped that such colleges will provide freedom to experiment, establish and develop educational programmes suited to the employment environment of the community in which it is located. Therefore, the curriculum is suitably designed to meet the needs of the local enterprises. The employers can also be involved in designing the curriculum. The instructors should maintain close contact with the officials of the local firms and get their advice not only on what skills are needed today but also what will be needed five to 10 years from now. Such institutions can also develop tailor-made training programmes in-house at a company or in the training institutions to meet the educational needs of the specific local enterprises.

Management of R&D for Industry–Academy Collaboration

In many countries, it is found that though heavy investment is made in technical education, equipment, infrastructure and computers, there is hardly adequate return in terms of development of applied research projects by which a country can benefit. In many cases it is found that the faculty of higher technical institutions are inclined to do basic research which helps them in publishing papers and enhancing their academic stature. However, this has not been usefully adopted by business and industry in the areas of applied research as they do not use sophisticated methodology. The result is that though there may be highly sophisticated institutions of technical education, they remain isolated pockets of excellence without much direct interaction with business and industry. Though these institutions are extremely well-equipped there is no platform where academics can share information with representatives from industrial houses and business enterprises. On the other hand, business enterprises lack the necessary infrastructure and facilities needed for research. Therefore, countries and institutions may consider establishing research parks' with the following guidelines:

1. Space in the institutions of excellence must be made available to industrial houses and business enterprises on lease basis with facilities for research;
2. Such facilities should form the nucleus of research parks with the most modern amenities and facilities;
3. These research parks should have a standing relationship with academicians for sharing of applied research results; and
4. The research parks should be managed by specially constituted committees appointed by the governing councils of the various institutions and should have representatives from different industries.

The expenses for establishing these research parks should be met out of the lease money on a time-bound basis and from other sources like charging for facilities provided to the industrial houses.

These research parks should be meant exclusively for applied research projects and should have no commercial objectives. These projects should have some relationship with the capabilities and potential of the concerned institution. The projects should utilise the faculties, libraries, equipment and other infrastructure in the institution. Some balancing arrangement of equipment and instruments for research should be made in the research parks. Industries and enterprises can have full rights to the products of such projects. However, the research methodology may be used by the academicians for teaching and publication purposes. Methodology and data collection can also be shared with other institutions. Such research parks have been established in the U.S. in as many as 80 institutions.[12]

Conclusion

Any HRD planning process must take into account the level of development of each country. Therefore, there cannot be uniform HRD strategies applicable to all situations. Even within the country, there could be wide variations in terms of the development of technology in different sectors of the economy. Though it is often argued that new markets and technologies require a more highly skilled, better educated, more mobile workforce, such statements may not hold for many developing countries given the employment level and opportunities available. There may be a shift from manual jobs to more white-collar ones. However, many workers are still struggling in a work environment which has not changed since the middle of the 18th century. Many more workers are caught up in the movement towards greater automation and at times perform mindless jobs; at the same time we may have some kind of technology importation.

Therefore, it may be impractical to assume that there will be sudden change of technology in all spheres in all countries. In certain segments and sectors, there may be modern technology, while in others, especially in the informal sector, traditional technology may continue with slight improvements. Therefore, we have to develop people with different training or different skills to suit the traditional and modern technologies besides a mix of the two.

HRD planning is closely related to the country's policies on choice of technology, the motivation level of the persons who will accept the change, the resistance from the trade unions, and the current educational level linked to the demand and supply of the workforce. Some of these issues have been discussed in other chapters.

Notes and References

1. Agricultural and Economic Research Centre, University of Delhi, 1986.
2. **Mehta, M.M.**, *Human Resources Development Planning*, Macmillan, Delhi, p. 7, 1976.

3. International Labour Organisation, *World Labour Report 1984: Vol. I*, Geneva, ILO, p. 188, 1984.

4. Ibid., p. 189.

5. Ibid., p. 148.

6. **Virmani, B.R.**, *Technology Transfer and Its Implications for Manpower Planning and Productivity*, Indian Council for Research on International Economic Relations, New Delhi, 1985.

7. **Mehta, M.M.**, see n. 2, p. 59.

8. **Virmani, B.R.**, *Graduate Engineer Trainees*, Administrative Staff College of India, Hyderabad, and FICCI, 1983.

9. **David, A.**, 'CAI: Yesterday, Today and Tomorrow', *Momentum*, p. 9, May 1978.

10. **Robinson, L.G.** and **Robinson, T.A.**, 'CAI in Health Education: A Pilot Study', *International Journal of Instructional Media*, Vol. 5, No. 3, 1977–78.

11. 'CAI: Who's in Control Here?', *Training HRD*, p. 54, September 1977.

12. *Fortune*, 11 May, 1987.

Additional References

Asian and Pacific Centre for Transfer of Technology of the UNESCAP, 'Technology Atlas—An Interim Report', *Asia-Pacific Tech Monitor*, March 1987.

Bhalla, Ajit S. and **James, Dilmus D.**, 'Technological Blending: Frontier Technology in Traditional Economic Sector', *Journal of Economic Issues*, Vol. XX, No. 2, June 1986, pp. 453–62.

Burrill, Steven, 'Managing the Technical', *Management Review*, American Management Association, December 1986.

Cascio, Wayne F. and **Awad, Elias M**, *Human Resources Management—An Information System Approach*, Reston Publishing Company, Reston, Virginia, 1981.

Dhesi, A.S., 'Aspects of Human Resource Development in India', *Social Science Research Journal*, Vol. II, No. 1&2, pp. 1–5, 1977.

Edquist, Charles, Jacobsson, Steffan and **Jethanandani, Kishore**, 'Automation in Engineering Industries of India and Republic of Korea against the background of experience in some OECD countries', *Economic and Political Weekly*, Vol. XX, No. 15, 13 April, 1985.

Hartmann, Gert. et al., 'Computerised Machine Tools, Manpower Consequences and Skill Utilisation', *British Journal of Industrial Relations*, Vol. XXI, No. 2, pp. 221–53, July 1983.

Harvey, James L., 'Effective Planning for Human Resources', *Personnel Administrator*, p. 45, October 1983.

Macklin, Thomas, 'Remodelling HRD', *Training and Development Journal*, p. 46–50, June 1982.

Tipton, Beryl, 'The Quality of Training and the Design of Work', *Industrial Relations Journal*, Vol. 13, No. 1, pp. 27–42, Department of Adult Education of the University of Nottingham, Spring 1982.

Virmani, B.R. and **Rao, Kala**, *Economic Restructuring, Technology Transfer and Human Resource Development*, Second Edition, Response Books, Sage Publications, New Delhi, 1999.

3

Corporate Planning and Training Strategy

Training has always been a necessary part of an organisation's efforts to recruit and effectively employ people in its ongoing processes. Because it is not always possible to recruit and properly assign individuals whose knowledge, attitudes and skills perfectly match the requirements of the job, training has been viewed as a means of closing the gap.

Training people to perform organisational tasks better is one thing; maintaining the organisation as an ongoing system is another. Neither by itself provides for effective adaptation to the changes induced by an organisation's environment and the corporate plans that directly affect its ability to accomplish its goals and to survive as a unified system. This deficiency has led to the conceptualisation of training as a formal organisational process with vastly different responsibilities and technologies.

Organisational training continues to be concerned with teaching particular skills for specific purposes, but its educational efforts are now directly connected with the role and working environment of the learner. Training has developed a more long-range orientation and is aimed at helping the organisation to adjust to the changing environment and emerging opportunities.

Training: A Corporate Activity

Not long ago, training was considered as an isolated activity, with which the top management or the corporate planners did not concern themselves. (It is still true, to an extent.) Except for occasional social interactions, there was hardly any contact between the trainer, the trainee and the top management. Part of the blame lies with the trainers because they viewed their function from a very narrow angle and did not really try to understand the totality of the organisation. The result was that the training function was given an inferior status that indirectly led to the recruitment and employment of staff of indifferent quality.

However, it is now realised that the present-day trainers must be a part of the mainstream of corporate activity. They should not think merely in terms of 'training the managers' but should instead offer solutions to management problems through a sound training strategy.

Interface between Corporate and Training and Development Plans

In order to examine the interface between corporate and business plans it is necessary to first examine the components and processes of business planning and see how they can be linked to training plans.

Corporate Planning

This is an activity that is concerned with the forward planning of the entire enterprise. Planning, to be realistic, must be based on the forward study of the present business situation and environment, and the factors that will influence its future. These factors can be broadly grouped into the following categories:

(a) Technological

(b) Product and market
(c) Resources (economic, financial, etc.)
(d) Personnel and organisational
(e) Environmental

It is important to remember that the dividing line between these factors may not always be clear cut. Overlapping is, in fact, inevitable in the planning process because, ultimately, the plan must contain all the factors to produce a composite picture. For example, if an organisation wants to go in for product diversifications, it will require new technology, it will need to invest in new machinery, develop a market demand, sell its product, modify or expand its organisation. Finally, to be able to put the plan into action, it has to find the manpower with the necessary skills at the right time, place and quantity. Therefore, it can be said that any objective that produces a change in one direction has its repercussions on most of the other elements of the organisation. And even if it does not affect some elements, it will invariably affect the manpower element. Therefore, manpower is a factor that cannot be overlooked in any corporate planning. It may be worthwhile to examine how this factor fits into the overall corporate activity of the organisation.

Manpower and Training Plans

An integrated approach to planning has been visualised earlier on the assumption that the business plan that emerges will take personnel factors into consideration along with other factors. Therefore, in any corporate manpower training and developmental plans, the following steps will have to be undertaken.

1. *Information on Business Plans and Objectives* This will be based on an analysis of the environment; determination of the key areas of activity, both now and in the future; devising a corporate strategy for achieving long term and short term goals. All the

manpower plans have to be linked to business plans and, therefore, one must perceive the changes likely to occur in the activities of the organisation. These could be:

(a) Changes in production and sales;
(b) changes in the nature of activities, i.e., marketing changes, method of distribution, customer changes, technological changes, etc.; and
(c) changes in the organisational activity, i.e., the organisation is either static, expanding or shrinking.

All these changes will have an implication on the quality and quantity of manpower requirements in the future.

2. *Organisational Analysis and Planning* This involves examining the strengths and weaknesses of the existing organisational structure, devising a structure capable of achieving the company's business plan, the manning pattern, work standards, among other things.

3. *Manpower Plans* These plans are concerned with all aspects of future manpower needs and working out the optimum means of obtaining these requirements. This will involve taking stock of the existing manpower, analysing future requirements and, by comparing the two, working out detailed staff requirements on the basis of time, quality and quantity dimensions.

4. *Recruitment and Placement Plan* This is concerned with matching organisational requirements with the existing manpower and acquiring what is not available with a focus on:

(a) The present structures that are weak and require intervention;
(b) the vertical and horizontal movement of managerial personnel as a result of which they may need to acquire knowledge, skills or behaviour patterns which they, at present, lack; and
(c) it will also bring into focus the training and developmental needs of the new personnel that will be inducted.

In many cases, this last aspect may become quite a critical factor and will require foresight and planning. To illustrate, suppose it was decided to start a factory in an area not providing the normal amenities and which did not have, in the immediate vicinity, personnel with the requisite qualifications. Assuming that these personnel were not available within the organisation, the only options would be either to recruit locally available talent and train them, which would be time consuming, or to get these personnel from the nearest place and then offer them extra wage incentives for agreeing to shift, which might have repercussions upon the company's wage bill and salary structure. In any event, training and development plans must aim at matching the people's skills, knowledge and behaviour to 'today's' job requirements and preparing them for the 'tomorrow's' job at the appropriate time.

An Action Plan

In order to link training plans to corporate projections, the following steps may be of help:

1. It is important to assess the likely levels and types of skills required in the future. This might mean forecasting for five to 10 years ahead. The main factors to consider are likely changes in technology, market trends, expansion plans, product changes and the introduction of new machines.

   From this, a broad assessment of the skills and knowledge required can be built up and a reasonable forecast made of the manpower needs. A pattern for training the new entrants and, wherever necessary, retraining the existing workers will then emerge. The age structure will have to be considered in designing the training activity.

2. Training should be work-centred and not person-centred. In other words, the work-related problems and difficulties should be identified as a first step in overcoming them.

3. Having made the assessment of future requirements, the management must next consider how to meet those requirements. It will be unwise to unilaterally design training

programmes and ask the employees to accept them. If any training activity, and the resultant organisational changes, are to be successful, these must be accepted by those affected by it. The acceptance will come more readily if those affected play a major part in creating a new structure.

One strategy could be the formation of a training committee to ensure that realistic plans are made and carried through. Such a committee must comprise senior line managers, the training officer as well as representatives of the supervisors and trade unions. The committee should consider the results of the study of organisation's future requirements and determine the best way to meet the organisation's need for knowledge and skill in the future. The organisation's training officer can act as an advisor but many new ideas and suggestions are likely to come from other members of the committee.

One of the fears often expressed by the management is that it is difficult to effect improvement because of opposition from trade unions. However, it must be understood that, by and large, trade unions may be ready to discuss changes in the training arrangement for managers and workmen provided such changes are likely to lead to improvement in the career prospects of those affected. Therefore, the management should try to ensure that trade union representatives are involved in any re-examination of the existing training and apprenticeship procedures. It is only then that there will be a better chance of effecting changes that will be in the best interest of the organisation and its employees.

4. The next stage will be to analyse the future knowledge and skill requirements in more detail so that a syllabus of learning needs can be drawn up. Part of the training syllabus will be specific and part will be a recognition of the organisation's needs to train employees in the habit of diagnosis and work planning.

5. The organisational recruitment plans should then be examined to determine if the types of persons recruited are likely

to have an aptitude for the required skill in which they are to be trained.

6. An outline of training courses could be drawn up for the organisation and implemented.

7. It is also important to ensure that the trainees are carefully coached and tutored throughout the period of training. There is little point in having a long and expensive period of training if much of it is spent without any structured guidance.

8. On-the-job training requires as much care and planning as any other training. Therefore, the training committee can suggest ways to impart on-the-job training.

9. Finally, the committee needs to study the procedures by which the total training efforts can be continuously evaluated and modified wherever necessary. It is important to stress here that organisations need to re-examine their present training system keeping in view the demands of the future and the changes likely to be effected in their plans. They should take into account the fact that the past skills, knowledge and the notions about training may not necessarily be valid for the future.

Corporate Training Strategy and Apprenticeship Schemes

It is important that any apprenticeship scheme (statutory or the organisation's own) be linked with the overall corporate plans. In the present-day context, there is always some sort of pressure from the trainees, specially those who are recruited under the statutory apprenticeship schemes, that they be employed by the training organisation. Therefore, as far as possible, the organisation should make an effort to see how it can link apprenticeship training with its own manpower requirements at present and in the future. Therefore, the stress on career planning and appropriate wage structure should form part of the corporate activity as well as training schemes. There are a number of organisations which do recruit the required number of trainees as per apprenticeship schemes. But they evolve their own career pattern and development schemes so that, as far as possible, these trainees get absorbed in the organisation.

Training and Organisational Philosophies

It is important that the training and the organisational philosophies must be in agreement with each other. If the organisation does not believe in implementing what is taught in training, then the trainees become critical of the training package being theoretical or irrelevant to the actual situation. Or they may become critical of their own organisation and lose faith in change because the organisation failed to bring about change and implement what they have learnt during training. This type of training has an adverse effect on the organisation.

Training Needs and Organisational Systems

Many of the organisational problems may be present because of lacunae in the organisational systems or policies. However, often the solution is sought in training with the result that such training does not result in any change. On the contrary, it only increases frustration. Therefore, while identifying training needs, it is important to first identify the issues and problems that are of concern to the organisation. The next exercise should be to see which problems can be tackled by changes in the system, wherever appropriate, and then see which are the problems which can be tackled by increasing the knowledge and skill of the personnel so that the training process can be designed to address such problems. In this process, training will be more realistic, will help solve some of the organisational issues and problems and get linked to the change process that is the most important objective of any training activity.

4

Evaluating and Measuring Management Training and Development

The importance of evaluation has been increasingly felt in the field of management education and development. In spite of this, there has been little systematic evaluation of management training and development programmes.

This chapter deals with various aspects of evaluation based on the Action Research approach followed by the author at the Administrative Staff College of India as part of his work on the evaluation of training and development sponsored by the Indian Council of Social Science Research (ICSSR).

The chapter emphasises the qualitative approach to the evaluation of learning in terms of knowledge, skills and attitudes and its subsequent transfer to the job. This has been done to identify the factors that seem to influence learning and indicate certain preconditions essential for training and developmental processes. An evaluation model, which needs to be incorporated in training and developmental activities, has been suggested. This model is based on the research methodology adopted by the research team comprising Ms Premila Verma and the author as project director.

Purpose of Evaluation

Any evaluation and measurement of management training and development can serve two important objectives. First is the impact of training. In other words, assessing whether the training has resulted in better performance by the trainees and brought about a change in attitude. The second objective of evaluation is to get a feedback about the relevance and usefulness of the training for those for whom it was intended. The objective here is to bring about an improvement in future developmental activities.

Where the first objective of measuring the impact of training is concerned, it is very difficult to do that in the short term. The trainees may come from different environments with different value systems. Therefore, it may be very difficult to measure the long-term impact of training. Moreover, the impact of any training can be known only in the course of time and not immediately. The implementation of any new idea depends upon a number of factors operating in an organisation. A training programme is only one such factor. In the absence of any change in the other factors, the training activity can have only a minimal impact. On the other hand, it may even lead to frustration among the trainees, if the training philosophy and the philosophy of the organisation are not in harmony. What is needed is a systematic study to develop reliable tools of evaluating the impact of training on the individual's performance. Therefore, the second objective—evaluation in terms of the relevance of the training activity, in order to improve future programmes—becomes important.

We are not only concerned with the evaluation of the training programme, but also its validation. Validation relates to the internal consistency of a training programme—whether it has achieved what it set out to do. We are concerned with validation in so far as it influences the evaluation of all the results of any training and development programme in the total management process—whether or not the original training design actually set out to achieve those results.

Randall[1] identified two main reasons for evaluation to be refined and to survive. Trainers who need to justify their existence and, thereby, to survive will be concerned with developing a methodology which can demonstrate the contribution which training has made in the past. To refine, on the other hand, involves learning from the past and putting that knowledge to use in training programmes in the future.

Trainees' Reaction and Training Objectives

Evaluation also presents a problem with regard to objectives of both the training programme and of the trainees. An objective evaluation system must be linked with the goals of the programme. Until there is a congruity of expectations, it is very difficult to measure the impact of a programme, especially if one relies exclusively on the reaction of the trainees. The immediate reaction of the trainees can be emotional, coloured by their own expectations from the training programme, which could be different from the expectations of the other trainees as well as the trainers. In one of the studies conducted by the author, the following observations were made:[2]

(a) Most of the trainees said that before undergoing training, they hardly thought about their reasons for attending training programmes. Most of them also said that their bosses never discussed why they were undergoing training with them.

(b) There was no uniformity in the trainees' expectations from the training programme. Each person's expectation was influenced by his/her own problems. The expectations also changed after the completion of training. Most of the trainees listed different objectives and expectations from that of the programme and these were not the same that they had stated before coming for training.

(c) And though the trainees' objectives and expectations from training did change after undergoing training, again there was no uniformity among them. They perceived their objectives in relation to their organisational situation and not in accordance with the objectives of the programme as stated by the trainers.

Therefore, in the absence of a congruence of goals, the success or failure of the programme should not be judged exclusively from the immediate reaction of the trainees. Such evaluations can be very subjective.

Moreover, training is considered to be an act of faith in the absence of proper goal congruence with regard to the expectations and objectives of the training. Normally, 'increased awareness in general outlook and approach' is the most frequently mentioned outcome of training. However, the trainees themselves are not clear about what exactly this means. The study also showed that there is no correlation between the reaction-based assessment on the post-training evaluation questionnaires and subsequent learning behaviour revealed in interviews long after the training. Neither was there any relationship between these assessments and subsequent expressions regarding the training.

The traditional validation approach to training assessment would have acted upon such immediate past training questionnaires and either wound up or radically altered training programmes which attracted such lukewarm response. We should, therefore, question whether this 'level of applause' criterion is an acceptable basis for training evaluation. The evidence of various studies is that such a criterion is highly suspect. The degree to which people criticise a training programme appears to bear no relationship to their subsequent learning from it. Therefore, the evaluation of various inputs must be related to the assessment of all the inputs—the content, method, environment, contributions, trainees—and not so much to the evaluation of the output.

Action-oriented Research Approach to Evaluation of Training and Development

It is, thus, obvious that till now no satisfactory scientific formula has been evolved to evaluate management development training.

It is still in the process of being worked out and a lot more experimentation and research is required before any definite conclusions can be drawn.

The process of evaluation in any sphere of activity is rarely thought of as an end in itself. It is usually seen as part of a larger process of attempting to bring about some change, make a choice, or take corrective action. Since evaluation is important for training, and since it cannot fulfil any function without affecting some large process, 'action research' approaches are particularly appropriate for evaluation studies and experiments.[3] There are two ways in which the 'action research' approach is different from other types of research approaches:

1. The results generated by 'action research' are used to influence the situation that is being researched.
2. The action researcher monitors the change brought about by his/her intervention in the research situation.

Design of the Action-oriented Evaluation Experiments

The basic objective of action-oriented evaluation experiments can be:

1. Working with the trainers and trying to work out what they are trying to achieve in terms of learning, and the consequences of this.
2. Trying to formulate some measure of whether such learning was achieved.
3. Applying such measures to training and relaying this information back to the trainers.
4. Any evaluation study of this nature will present some problems especially if one of the indices chosen is the trainees' perception of what they have learnt from the parts of the training design. This should not necessarily be held to be an index of performance, but it can be held to be an important variable, since the trainees' perceptions of how much they

have learnt is likely to affect the extent to which they try to apply what they have learnt.

5. The trainers do not get a feedback about their training inputs until after the trainees had experienced it on the training programme that was studied; any effect of such a feedback will be seen when the input is repeated in the next programme. It should therefore be concluded that if the research influencing evaluation procedures has any beneficial effects, this will be reflected in higher average ratings later.

Evaluation as a Part of the Developmental Process

Management training and development is an important part of organisational development. Determination of the effectiveness of the training programmes will not only lay the foundation for further progress, but will also show whether the investments in terms of time, money and energy have yielded the desired results to the organisation. Since the initial phase of training begins much before the trainee enters the scene, the evaluation of the effectiveness of training must be a part of the total training activity. Hence the plan for evaluation has to precede training and not follow it.

Once evaluation is accepted as part of training then,

(a) It has to be consistent with the purposes, objectives and goals of the training activity;

(b) It needs to be a continuous process (the 'one-shot' appraisal without appropriate analysis, follow-up and reappraisal will make it impossible to establish a sound basis for improvement); and

(c) Evaluation has to be specific to the training activity. Generalisations drawn from one training programme may provide a broad basis for improvement, but training evaluation has to be tailored to fit particular training programmes. Therefore, there is a need for the trainers to insist on a complete and detailed evaluation to get a continuous feedback relating to the progress and the problems faced by trainees in order to maintain the momentum of the training programme, its evaluation and subsequent improvement.

A functional definition of 'training' has been given as the acquisition of knowledge, skills and attitudes; and the term 'development' has been used to denote its application to the job for improving the organisation.

Evaluation Model[4]

The training programme constitutes a three-stage system. The first stage is the period 'before' the learning experience during which the trainee has certain expectations from the training. The second is the teaching or learning stage. The third is when the learner, back on the job, is supposed to have integrated the training with his job performance.

Incorporating the three stages of training in the evaluation model is shown in Figure 4.1.

Pre-training Evaluation

Assessment of Training Objectives of the Trainee and His/Her Boss

Much of what the individual gains through training depends on his/her perceptions about training, his/her existing state of knowledge and attitude and potential for improvement. As already mentioned, managements are vague about the objectives of training. The objectives of the boss may differ from those of the trainee, which in turn may not concur with the training objectives. This lack of goal congruence becomes a major problem because critical evaluation of the achievements of any training has to be done in the light of the objectives intended to be achieved.

Thus, assessment of the training objectives of the trainees and their bosses before they come for training should be the first step

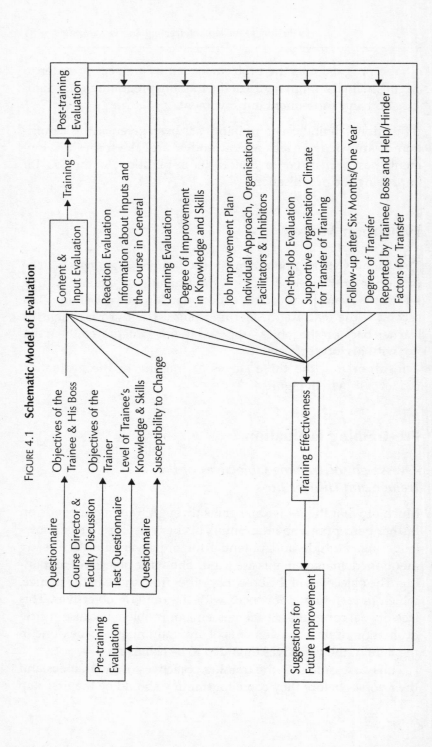

FIGURE 4.1 **Schematic Model of Evaluation**

to achieving goal congruence. In one study by the author, this was done by sending a questionnaire to the trainees and their bosses. The bosses were requested to indicate the department's needs and expectations from the training programme. The trainees were requested to specify their expectations from the training in terms of their individual and organisational needs.

A pre-evaluation study of this type helps avoid situations where the trainee says, 'I am here because my boss sent me' or 'My boss does not know why I am here.' It creates an awareness in the organisation about the needs of training. It is quite possible that during the process of pre-training, the management feels the need to discuss the objectives of training with the trainee. Such a discussion may help overcome the perception gap of trainee's needs and organisational needs. The trainees can also become more realistic about their expectations from training. This is the first step towards motivation for learning. Goal congruence, thus, does not merely remain an evaluation issue but becomes a part of training.

Test of Knowledge, Skills and Attitudes   The second part of the pre-training task evaluates the trainee's existing state of knowledge and skills and the attitude towards various management concepts in order to draw comparisons and measure changes brought about by training. The existing level of knowledge of the trainee will help in deciding the level at which the trainer starts teaching in order to ensure that trainees do not feel they already are familiar with the subject. In the study by the author, a test questionnaire was prepared covering the course inputs, and the scores so obtained indicated the trainee's existing level of knowledge and skills before the training.

Each trainer prepared the questionnaire with objective-type questions on the basis of the inputs he/she planned to give in the programme.

Since most management training programmes also aim at modifying the trainee's attitudes towards various management concepts, an assessment of the attitudinal changes had to be done. The important question here is the degree of susceptibility to change among the trainees. A standardised scale was prepared to measure the trainee's degree of change and adaptability to new work situations. This scale was administered as a part of the test questionnaire.

Input Evaluation

Pre-training evaluation will not only help the management and the trainee in identifying training needs but will also help trainers to become more acquainted with the diverse training needs of individual trainees.

The trainers need to assess how far their training inputs contribute to the achievement of training objectives. The effects of training cannot be judged unless the inputs are in conformity with the objectives of the programme.

In order to evaluate their own inputs, the trainers should judge beforehand whether their inputs will result in enduring learning, and how far it will influence the trainees' subsequent work performance. In a nutshell, the trainer should assess the suitability of his/her own inputs.

These various steps in the pre-training stage are important not only for an objective evaluation of training but also for improving trainees' learning. An interesting study by Warr, Bird and Rackham showed that in respondents who had undergone training and answered a pre-training test questionnaire, there was a 65 per cent improvement in the post-training test questionnaire, as against an improvement of 37 per cent in those executives who underwent training only. This shows that the pre-training questionnaire increases the trainee's awareness about the various management concepts before the training itself and increases his/her motivation to learn.

Post-training Evaluation

Reaction Evaluation

Soon after training, the trainees' reactions are obtained through an evaluation proforma that elicits information about the course inputs and the impression about the training in general.

The trainers' observation of the trainees' reactions during discussions form another useful, though not a very objective, device for evaluating training. From the reaction evaluation the trainer is able to gauge the frame of mind of the trainee. If a trainee leaves with a negative reaction towards the training, he will hardly be motivated to learn or, even if something is learnt, he may not be committed to transfer it to the job situation.

Learning Evaluation

The test questionnaire, which is prepared for assessing trainees' knowledge and skills before training, is administered again at the end of the course. It measures the degree of learning acquired through the programme by calculating the change in pre-training and post-training scores.

Job-improvement Plan

The aim of training is improved performance on the job. Evaluation of the trainee's performance while he/she is still in the training institution poses a problem to the evaluator because improvement is sought to be measured without providing an opportunity for the training to be put into practice. Other problems that confront the evaluator are the nature and diversity of management tasks; the different manner in which managers do the same job; and the same manager doing the same job, adopting different skills on different occasions.

One of the techniques attempted to overcome these problems is the preparation of a job-improvement plan. This is an action plan prepared by each participant for improving his/her job-performance on the basis of what has been learnt during the training. The job-improvement plan involves:

1. Analysis of the standard of performance in the trainee's organisation with reference to each input area discussed during training.
2. Planning the action, step-by-step, on the basis of the requirements of his/her own organisation for bringing about improved functioning.

3. Determination of the target date within which the planned change can be put into action and the co-operation expected from various levels in the organisation.
4. Highlighting organisational facilitators and inhibitors that the trainee visualises while implementing his action plan.

Preparation of the job-improvement plan by each individual is a good opportunity for planning the transfer of training to the job by enabling him/her to do the following:

1. Providing an opportunity to the trainee in evaluating his/her own learning.
2. Enabling the trainee to perceive the relevance of the training for the job.
3. Providing an opportunity to adopt advanced management concepts and techniques in day-to-day functions.
4. Helping in identifying conditions in the organisation which will help or hinder the transfer of training to the job.
5. Helping in finding suitable ways of overcoming these conditions.
6. Lastly, encouraging the trainee to return to the organisation with confidence, commitment and with a positive attitude towards introducing changes.

Thus, the job-improvement plan is not merely a tool for evaluation but becomes an important element in the learning process.

On-the-job Evaluation Unless the implementation of the job-improvement plan is verified, its preparation is not justified. This step is not purely evaluative, but needs to be integrated with the training process since it involves gathering information about the constraints in the transfer of training and facilitating such transfer. The organisation can be asked to re-brief the trainee on his/her return about the learning and the improvements he/she envisages. The boss can even encourage the trainee to further modify, change or delete certain aspects of job-improvement plan in the light of the organisational requirements. This kind of discussion is likely to increase the receptivity of the organisation to new ideas acquired through training.

Follow-up after Six Months/One Year   The training institution is interested in the transfer of the knowledge acquired during training to the job. The progress of the executive is normally monitored through follow-up. The follow-up, done either through questionnaires or through personal interviews, consists of checking on the implementation of the action plan prepared by the executive. To ensure a more conducive climate for introducing changes, it is desirable to involve the trainee's boss at the follow-up stage also. The boss may be asked to cite instances of where the trainee has implemented changes.[5]

The Action-oriented Research Approach to Evaluation

Benefits

This approach to evaluation can be beneficial in the following ways:[6]

1. It will help in stimulating the trainers to think through the rationale for their activities, and also provide them with some knowledge of the results.
2. It will also enable the trainees to think about their expectations from the training programme and how it is related to their job situation.
3. This will help in managing management development programmes by providing the much-needed feedback and to keep an effective control over input design and its consequences.
4. Lastly, there is one benefit that extends beyond the situation in which it is carried out. The direct influence of such evaluation can be viewed as a general technique for improving management development systems.

Difficulties in this Approach

The criteria of the action-oriented research approach to evaluation can be difficult in the initial stages. There is a possibility of resistance from the trainers as it will require a lot of introspection in terms of developing a rationale for the input. This will also involve the trainer devising a criterion for the evaluation of the relevance of his/her own input. Self-questioning can always be a painful process. However, in the long run, it is likely to pay much more dividends in not only adding to evaluation research but also helping to bring about goal congruence between the learners and the trainers.

Notes and References

1. **Randal, L.K.**, 'Evaluation—A training dilemma', *Journal of the American Society of Training Directors*, Vol. 14 (5), pp. 29–35, 1960.
2. **Virmani, B.R.**, *Training of Senior Executives: Objectives and Achievements*, Oxford Centre for Management Studies, Oxford, pp. 1–10, 1975.
3. **Burgoyne, J.G.**, 'New Approach to Evaluating Management Programmes', *Personnel Review (4)*, pp. 40–44, 1973.
4. This model is based on the research methodology adopted by the research team at the Administrative Staff College of India.
5. **Warr, P., Bird, M.M.** and **Rackham, N.**, *Evaluation of Management Training—A practical framework, with cases, for evaluation, training needs and results*, Gower Press, London, 1970.
6. **Virmani, B.R.** and **Seth, Premila**, *Evaluation of Management Training and Development—An Action Research Approach*, All India Management Association, New Delhi, 1978.

Additional References

Virmani, B.R. and **Seth, Premila**, *Evaluating Management Training and Development*, Vision Books, New Delhi, 1985.

Virmani, B.R., 'Human Resources for Advancement of Management Education' in Vinayshil Gautam (Ed.), *Learning Management*, Allied Publishers Ltd, New Delhi, pp. 75–85, 1996.

5

Management Training and Development: An Evaluation Approach

Over the last two decades, there has been greater awareness regarding management training and development in all the sectors of the Indian economy. As a result, there has been a growing need to find ways to determine the efficiency and effectiveness of management training and development activity from the point of view of organisational improvements. However, in spite of this, there has been little systematic emphasis on evaluation to enhance the process of management development. To fill this gap, a longitudinal study of management training and development and their evaluation was undertaken. The research study was divided into two phases. The first phase dealt with the transfer of learning in the training institution; and the second related to the transfer of learning to the job. This chapter deals with some of the findings of the second phase of the study.

The study aimed at:

1. Analysing the impact of management training and development programmes, if any;

2. Evolving suitable criteria for checking the application of training inputs in order to equip the trainees for the specific needs of their sponsoring organisations;
3. Exploring and correlating various organisational factors that help/hinder the transfer of training to the job; and
4. To study, given the adequacy and applicability of training inputs directed towards the development of the manager, the tangible benefits to the sponsoring organisation, if any.

The selection of the trainees was confined to selected programmes conducted by the Administrative Staff College of India (ASCI). In addition, for case studies, the data was collected through questionnaires from trainees representing over 30 organisations, while five organisations were chosen for an in-depth study. In the case of training in government-run training institutions, the data was collected from heads/faculty of 30 such institutions. In addition, trainees from various government departments were interviewed separately, including ministers and secretaries to the Government of India who had come to attend training programmes at ASCI. The initial data was collected through questionnaires which was later followed up with in-depth interviews. During the interviews, it was found that interviewees' responses differed from their answers to the mailed questionnaires. Therefore, the major emphasis was subsequently shifted to interviews and the filling up of the questionnaires by the researchers.

A multi-pronged data collection methodology was adopted which included—apart from interviews and questionnaires—observations, in-depth case studies of selected organisations, case studies of individual trainees, group discussions among trainees and follow-up of job improvement plans prepared by the trainees. All the tools used for measuring the transfer of learning were administered at least six to 12 months after training. Both quantitative and qualitative approaches were adopted to the analysis of data.

The Training Function

Of late, most organisations have been feeling the need to have a full-fledged, separate, training set-up called either the training or the HRD department or the organisation development department. The major function of the training department is either.to organise in-company training programmes or sponsor executives for external training programmes.

Earlier, in many organisations there was a feeling that the persons manning the training departments have been transferred from various other line and staff functions because they were not considered very competent in their own areas. However, this trend is now gradually changing in some of the organisations. It was also found that the trainers were not happy in the training department and, barring a few exceptions, a majority of them were looking forward to being posted to their original departments, with the result that little effort was made to develop their skills as trainers. The trainers perceived their role more in terms of the administrative aspects of training. For example, in in-company management development programmes, they perceived their role as limited to arranging the faculty (external and internal), preparing the timetable and making other administrative arrangements. In the case of external training programmes, they played a minor role in identifying training needs; instead, they confined themselves to getting nominations from various departments and sponsoring executives for external programmes and corresponding with the training institutions. Also, most of the executives interviewed did not have a high opinion of the training department and saw it more as handling the administrative aspect of training.

The Status of the Training Department

This differs from organisation to organisation. In some cases, the head was equivalent to the level of a deputy general manager which, in most organisations, ranks lower than the head of the personnel function; while in other cases, the position was still lower, to the level of middle or lower-middle management.

Identification of Training Needs

It was interesting to find that though the budget for training has been increasing and there is greater awareness about training, very little effort has gone into a systematic identification of training needs.

In a large number of cases, training needs identification was perceived as an ad hoc affair. This was especially true of the government departments where neither the trainee nor his/her boss was consulted. For example, in one large organisation, the executives were ordered to attend a particular programme just a few days before. In spite of their reluctance to go, they were threatened with disciplinary action and forced to go. A major complaint from government officials was that many of the courses selected were not relevant to their job. In some cases, a person was nominated twice, within a span of two years for a programme on the same subject. The subject was neither connected to the person's current job nor was likely to be helpful in his future job. This led to a lot of hostility towards, and cynicism about, training. As a result, trainees started perceiving training more as a paid holiday or a junket than as a means to learn something new.

Coming to the tools for the identification of training needs, most organisations have a column in the annual appraisal report with regard to training needs. However, in reality, it was found that in most cases the appraisal reports were rarely consulted while taking training decisions; and even if they were, not much weightage was given to them. Part of the problem was also with regard to the column in the appraisal report. In most cases, it mentioned the names of the courses, or at times the institutes or places of training which had very little relevance to the strengths and weaknesses of executives as revealed in the first part of the appraisal about result achievement or work performance.

However, in government departments and a few public sector organisations, the personnel/training department arbitrarily decided on the training programmes needed, without consulting the appraisal report, the trainee or his boss. For example, one person working for a tourism department was sent for a programme on urban development twice. In another case, a person dealing with development administration was sent for training relating to marketing. The assumption here was that they might get posted to some of these areas in the future. However, the officials interviewed felt that the chances of such postings were very remote and if at all they did materialise, it may not be in the near future. They would have liked at least part of the training to be linked to their present job or to the job to which they were likely to be posted in the near future.

There were also cases where the training needs identification exercise was done when it was necessary to groom people for higher responsibilities. In other words, training was linked to promotion. However, even here there were instances where the trainees found the training was not relevant to their future jobs and they saw it more as an additional reward before promotion.

Where the training needs identification and appraisal for promotion were combined, there was always an apprehension in the minds of both the executives and their bosses that any deficiencies expressed under the training needs identification would be seen as signs of weakness and adversely affect prospects of promotion. Therefore, in most cases, the executives and their bosses were guarded in their remarks about these deficiencies.

In public sector and government organisations, sponsoring of executives for training is linked to the budget. Since the budget for training has increased considerably, often there is pressure, particularly towards the end of the financial year, to send more personnel for training. So officials were sent for training without considering the specific training requirements. As a result, training was often perceived as a waste of money and it also gave rise to a negative attitude towards training and change. Where training and the organisational philosophy were at variance and the executives, after training, could not bring about any change due to lack of organisation support, it only resulted in greater frustration with the job or the organisation. This also led to cynicism about any change.

Selection of Trainees

In the course of the study, various reasons/criteria for selection came to our notice. In one organisation, certain courses were earmarked for every executive who completed a minimum period of service and then, based on seniority and the budget, executives were sponsored for further training automatically, irrespective of their training needs, the usefulness or the relevance of the training programmes to their respective areas of work. This was illustrated by a typical statement of one of the trained managers who said that although a systematic selection procedure was chalked out, it was limited to paper alone and was not put into practice. Neither the trainee, nor his boss was consulted on the training needs and the selection was done arbitrarily by the personnel department or by the various heads of departments in the organisation.

Where the training was linked to promotion, it was perceived more as an incentive or bonus than as a means of strengthening the trainees' potential and supplementing their knowledge. In such instances, the training needs of the organisations were not clear but it did not matter much to the trainees.

In another organisation, the selection procedure, especially for external courses, was considered as an incentive to perform better after training; while in yet another case, it was considered a paid holiday and relief from routine work. There were also instances where there were systematic selection procedures but the selected executives could not be spared from work and others who could be were sent to the training course instead. One organisation preferred to send only the younger managers for training, which created a lot of disharmony among the executives.

One of the common methods of training needs identification and selection of trainees, is the circulation of the training brochure (for internal as well as external training programmes) to various departments and inviting nominations. The departmental heads, normally on the basis of their own judgement or on the initiative of the executives themselves, nominate people for different training programmes. The training department, depending on the budget, sends the nominated executives for training. If all the aspiring executives cannot be accommodated, then a priority list is prepared and the selected candidates are sent as and when funds are available. In such cases, very little effort is made to link training with the needs of the particular individual, the department or the organisation.

In one organisation, one of the top executives was invited by a training institution as a guest lecturer. The training institution also sent a few brochures to the executive, with a request to send a few nominations for the programme. The executive, in turn, sent the brochures to the training department. It was pointed out that none of the executives suitable for that programme were available and those who were available may not be suitable for that programme. The training department, however, was pressurised to send any three executives regardless of their suitability. Similar instances were quoted in another organisation also. In all such cases, the selection of participants for training had absolutely no relevance to the training needs identification.

There were a few organisations which adopted a systematic procedure. In one organisation, there was a systematic identification of potential and training programmes were selected and executives were sent for them on the basis of that study. However, one organisation did this only so long as it was a multinational. After its nationalisation, the procedure was given up.

Budget for Training

Most of the organisations studied, especially those in the public sector, had a formal training budget. In recent times, the budget for training has been increasing. However, in many organisations, the budget was decided first and the selection of trainees was done later; while it should have been the other way around, that is, the training needs should have been identified first, based on which the budget should have been prepared.

In some government organisations, there was a clear directive that every executive must undergo a training programme once a year and that the budget for training must be utilised. There was an interesting case of a particular executive who was sponsored for an external programme but his name was rejected for the course by the training institution. A telex message was immediately sent to the training institution, that as per the directive of the Prime Minister every government executive had to be accepted for that particular training programme or for any other training programme in the institution and that the executive would be reaching the training institution irrespective of whether he is accepted or not!

In some organisations, the budget was strictly adhered to, while in a few cases, the budget was not only flexible but also factored in inflation. In a few cases, though the budget was meant for training, it was understood that the training would be more of a reward. In some cases, the training budget could not be utilised for training at all because it always took a second place to the exigencies of work.

Selection of Courses

The selection process for the external training programmes was normally based on the reputation of the training institution and its faculty, the facilities available, the feedback from the earlier training programmes and, at times, the relevance of the course to the organisation's needs. In some cases, the location of the training institution also counted. For example, when there was an adequate budget, locations like hill stations were preferred even if the course was not entirely relevant.

The most common methodology adopted in choosing a training programme was by circulation of the brochures and recommendations of the departmental head. In certain cases, especially in the government, the executive was given two or three options of courses to choose from, and then nominated for one of the courses. Training in foreign locations was always treated as a reward.

Pre-course Preparation

In most of the organisations studied, there was hardly any pre-course preparation. In many cases, the trainees were neither aware of the training programme, nor of the reasons for their selection or about the content or objectives of the training programme. In some cases, though the training material was sent in advance by the training institutions, the trainees hardly got the time to read them. Often they did not even get to see the course brochures. In some cases, where selection was done without prior notice, it led to resentment on the part of the trainees against the training programme as well as their organisation. There was hardly time to even think of pre-course preparation.

However, in one private sector organisation, there was a systematic pre-course preparation. The executive was released from his normal work at least one week in advance so that he could visit the various departments of the organisation, understand their functioning and problems. The trainees were also given books related to the programme by the training department so that they could familiarise themselves with the subjects. Of course, one of the objectives of such an elaborate procedure, as stated by the organisation, was to ensure that the executives projected a good image of the organisation. In the process, it was found that there was greater receptivity of the training inputs as well as commitment to transfer the learning to the job later on.

Learning and Transfer of Learning

Any training activity has two aspects: one is learning in the training institution and the other is the transfer of that learning to the job. So far as learning in the training context is concerned, the most common tool used is the perception of the participants as to how much they would learn from specific inputs. However, in our earlier studies, we found that the participants' immediate perception was not a reliable tool and other methods for measuring the transfer of learning like pre-training and post-training questionnaires, job-improvement plans, and feedback after a time gap were devised. Our case studies showed that although a positive feedback was given immediately after the course, over a period of time a lot that was taught was found to be irrelevant, especially in the service industry. For example, in the case of the banking sector, the trainees found that many of the inputs of external programmes did not relate to their situation; where they did, it was like a refresher course rather than any addition to their knowledge. Yet, the executives were sponsored for such external training programmes on a regular basis. What this probably reveals is that the training was treated more as a reward or, in some cases, the executives were sent to such programmes to get an insight into the working of other industries. The training, though not directly relevant, had some indirect benefits like change of atmosphere from the regular work routine, getting to know people of other organisations, and a free holiday which in the process added to their general knowledge.

Apart from the direct benefits of training in the form of additional knowledge and skills, training helped develop the confidence of the trainees. The course inputs of training programmes were not only directly related to the trainee's area of work but were also general in nature and helped the trainees view their organisation's problems in totality, improved their attitude and enhanced their decision-making skills.

In certain instances, the training institution asked the trainees to prepare job-improvement plans at the end of the course, which was followed up later on. In such cases, training did result in some steps to improve the performance and also led to a positive perception of training by the trainee, his boss and the organisation. However, in some other instances, where the job improvement plan was prepared, either there was no follow-up or the trainee was immediately transferred to some other function not related to the training.

Most of the benefits of the transfer of learning were seen in the case of functional management programmes rather than general management programmes. There were also instances where the transfer of learning was more effective after a time gap, when the participants had an opportunity to implement what they had learnt.

In organisations where there was no systematic effort for the transfer of learning, there was a 'relapse' to the older ideas. If this happens in a large number of cases, then in due course of time, organisations cease to change. This phenomenon can be partly due to the fault of the trainers. When they discuss any organisational aspects and change, they must take into account the kind of resistance the trainees might face while implementing such changes and prepare them to overcome such resistance. The organisations are also to blame, because they believed in training but not necessarily in change or in the implementation of what their executives had learnt.

It was also found that the transfer of learning was greater in the case of in-company programmes mainly because the training inputs were geared to the needs of the organisation. In another case, because a large number of people in the organisation were put through similar training, they all understood and appreciated the implications of the change and it then became easier to implement the changes in the organisation. In the case of external training programmes, as only a few executives could be trained at a time, there was always resistance from others to bringing about changes.

Factors that Help or Hinder Transfer of Learning to the Job

Various factors could facilitate or hinder the transfer of learning to the job. Some of these are: the organisational climate, support received from the top management, colleagues and subordinates and the attitude of the trainee and his/her boss towards training.

Organisational Factors

In one of the case studies, it was found that a total change in the organisational set-up led to a lot of disharmony and redundancy, resulting in resistance to any change. However, after the reorganisation, there was a gradual streamlining of the distribution and delegation of authority and the trainees felt that they had greater freedom to put their learning into practice. Lack of communication between various levels in the organisational set-up was also cited as a hindrance factor.

Organisational climate played a major role in the transfer of training to the job. The major organisational climate components mentioned were indifference of the superiors, peers and subordinates towards the trained executives and deliberate efforts to obstruct any change.

Rigid Rules and Conservativeness of the Organisation

Other organisational climate factors, which prevented the transfer of learning were rigid rules and regulations, lack of freedom to introduce change and lack of encouragement for innovation. In actual practice, it was found that the transfer of training was possible where the trainee proceeded with determination, was able to manipulate the situation to change, and especially if he/she had a good record, created a favourable impression about his/her work in the organisation and had a good relationship with the management and colleagues. In other words, personal goodwill played a major role.

Relevance of Training

In the service organisations studied, it was noticed that often the training was irrelevant, the selection of courses had no rationale and, therefore, no transfer of learning could be effected. There were also instances of executives who had earlier reported that the training was irrelevant and useless, changing their stand later and saying that they were able to change their attitude and transfer some of the training to the job.

Management's Attitude to Changes

In one organisation, the absence of rigid rules and regulations and a culture of allowing the freedom to introduce innovative changes had helped in the process of the transfer of learning. The proper identification of training needs and proper selection of courses also helped in a big way. On the other hand, selection based on criteria such as influence with the management, subjective judgement of meritorious performance and whether an executive can be spared at the time of training did affect the interest and motivation of the trainees to learn, with the result that the transfer of learning was minimised.

Training of Critical Mass

Another factor in the transfer of learning was the training of the critical mass. The transfer was greater when a large number of executives were sent for similar training, than when only a selected few were sent. There were cases where a number of people who attended a particular programme in the same institution, developed a camaraderie, resulting in improved interpersonal relations, which, in turn, greatly reduced inter-departmental clashes, and, consequently, greater support to the transfer of learning to the job.

Among the other hindrances mentioned were union resistance, government interference and, over-centralisation of decision-making.

Evaluation of Training and Development

Since organisations spend a lot of money, time and effort in training, they are naturally keen on finding out whether it resulted in trainees learning anything new, but also the subsequent transfer of this learning to the job situation. In most cases, the organisations studied did not have a proper evaluation system. At the most, the trainee was asked to give a report about how useful the training was; if the participants gave a favourable report about the course then it was assumed that the training was useful. In some organisations, the intention of evaluation was mainly to determine the utility of the course in the perception of the executives in order to decide whether more executives should be sponsored to the same course or the same institution in future. There were also cases where the trainees did not give a negative feedback though they found the course irrelevant. This was attributed to the executives' concern that they should not spoil their colleagues' chances for a sort of 'paid holiday'. There was the fear that an unfavourable report could reflect upon the executive's own capacity to learn. In the case of government, it was revealed that in some instances a confidential report on trainees was sought from the training institution in order to give an adverse feedback about training, which in turn could spoil their career prospects. Therefore, they tended to give a positive feedback even if they felt that the training did not result in much learning.

There were also a few cases where the executives were asked to give a thorough feedback about the training programme listing the benefits and the drawbacks. The evaluation of the programme by the executives was given due weightage. The utility of training was also assessed in terms of the job-improvement plan. Subsequently, if it was found necessary, the executives were made to undergo another training programme to reinforce their learning and to refresh their knowledge. In certain cases, the preparation of the job-improvement plan also helped the training institution in terms of measuring the effectiveness of training and, based on this, subsequent training programmes were modified.

In-company Training Programmes

Both in-company and external training programmes have their advantages and disadvantages. However, if used with discretion, they can complement each other.

External training programmes are generally more helpful in cases where the trained executives are expected to act as change agents in the organisation, especially where attitudinal change is the major focus. There is an opportunity for interacting with a diverse group of people and a spontaneous exchange of ideas and feelings, giving the executives an insight into the functioning of other organisations. In the process, the trained executives develop confidence and, through peer pressure, they tend to accept different ideas and new systems for implementation in their own organisations.

The main utility of in-company programmes lies in training a critical mass of personnel in a subject concerning the organisation. Such training programmes provide a common platform for the executives of the organisation to meet, exchange views and understand each other's role in the organisation leading to its smoother functioning. Such training also helps to tackle the specific problems and issues of the organisation. But there is hesitancy about opening up in in-company training either due to the office hierarchy or concern for colleagues' feelings. As a result, concrete attitudinal or behavioural changes are not possible.

In terms of cost effectiveness of training programmes, in-company training was reported to be more economical. But the cost effectiveness was measured only in terms of the number of executives trained at a time, rather than the qualitative impact of training, or the amount of knowledge acquired and transferred to the work environment.

The internal programmes are ideally intended to be more specific in nature, relating to particular functions and issues of the organisation, reinforcing the existing potential of the executives and strengthening their weak points. As a result, the executives should be well equipped to tackle the specific problems within the organisation.

The content of the external programmes is more general in nature, providing new knowledge and ideas and a wider perspective. Therefore, although not directly related to problem solving, external programmes help executives analyse a situation in its totality. Due to the confidence gained through training, the risk-taking ability of the executives is enhanced and, at times, they are in a better position to visualise and also bring about desirable changes in the organisation.

The one major disadvantage of an external programme, often noticed, was that the course contents can not be planned taking into account each individual's organisational background. Moreover, the capacity of the participants to grasp the inputs differed.

Most executives preferred external training to internal training, first, because of the prestige attached to selection for external training which may be linked to promotion, and second, because the training gives them a break from regular work. In some cases, external training was preferred for the quality of the course content.

In the case studied we tried to elicit information regarding the objectives, processes and impact of in-company training programmes as against the external training. Although, in-company training can be most beneficial to organisations, resulting in optimum impact, there were major weaknesses in their operation which have been analysed.

In-company Training Department

In most of the large organisations studied, there were in-company training centres with reasonably good infrastructure and training staff. However, in reality, they assumed a purely administrative role, limited to selecting participants for training in consultation with the heads of departments, designing the curriculum, selecting the faculty and making all other arrangements for training programmes. The training centre personnel were rarely trainers themselves and there was no training scheme for improving the skills of the trainers.

In-company Training Faculty

In organisations where the training department personnel were themselves the trainers it was found that most of the personnel were from line functions, who were disinterested in improving training. Some trainers who sincerely tried to contribute to training were transferred back to their functions in no time and in the few instances where they were not transferred it was mainly because they were not wanted back. As a result, the training department personnel were in a constant state of flux and they were seen as stop-gap arrangements.

In-company training programmes relied greatly on external faculty, who were selected on the basis of their qualifications and reputations, rather than their ability to relate the training to the organisation's problems. The training, therefore, only gave a theoretical perspective. In most cases the external faculty was not even briefed about the training design, objectives and organisational problems.

Types of Internal Training

In all the cases studied, the in-company training consisted of various types of induction programmes for the new employees, with a view to exposing them to organisational policies. In addition, there were functional programmes and some organisations also had general management programmes.

Selection of Participants for In-company Training

The selection of trainees for internal programmes was normally done in consultation with the executive, his/her superior and the training department. In some organisations, training was compulsory for all executives, irrespective of their training need. When selection was based on individual merit, it was considered a matter of prestige. However in some organisations, selection for training was considered an indication of the executive's inefficiency.

In-company Training Design

It is often assumed that an in-company training programme will automatically take into consideration the organisation's goals and problems and ensure that the training is effectively utilised in the company's progress. But, in reality, it was found that curriculum designs are not effectively geared towards organisational problems. The course material does not have much bearing on the issues concerning the organisation and the topics to be covered were left to the discretion of the faculty.

Impact of In-company Training

Since in-company training exposes large number of executives in the organisation to similar kind of training, simultaneously, the executives tend to think alike, and co-operate in transferring learning to the job effectively, to achieve common organisational goals.

The various lacunae in in-company training meant that it did not serve the purposes of improving the efficiency of executives or helping the company progress.

Factors that Help/Hinder in Transfer of In-company Training

Participants in in-service training programmes can neither be disinterested nor irresponsible during the programme. Factors which hinder the transfer of learning of external programmes to the job like rigid organisational policies, resistance and apathy of superiors, colleagues and subordinates were minimised in the case of in-training programmes.

But the lack of proper in-company training design with suitable faculty is a major hindrance, first in acquiring knowledge and second, since the inputs were not really geared to the organisational issues, in the transfer of learning to the job.

Evaluation and Follow-up of In-company Training

Perhaps due to the lacunae in the effective conduct of in-company training, most organisations did not conduct any kind of evaluation of the training. In the rare instances where an evaluation was done, it was limited to a feedback about whether trainees liked the sessions or not. No information was sought regarding the actual learning, its relevance and applicability to the job. No job-improvement plans were prepared and, most often, the training was forgotten after the end of the course and no follow-up done.

Although massive amounts of money are invested in in-company training, there is no cost-benefit analysis done to ensure that the investment was utilised fruitfully. Evaluation of a training programme especially an in-company one should therefore be built into the training policy.

Transfer of Learning—Some Suggestions

In the study it was found that learning and its transfer were linked to various organisational factors and individual disposition of the trainees. Where there was a positive attitude towards training, there was greater absorption of learning and its subsequent transfer to the job. There was also greater commitment where the trainee was involved in his selection and was sent in preparation for higher responsibilities. However, in many cases, the trainees were sent for training as a general policy without any identification of their training needs.

When asked what they had learnt, most trainees spoke in very vague and general terms like having developed a better understanding of the managerial role and requirements or that they got an opportunity to compare the managerial styles of other organisations. Where the training was based on proper training needs identification, the trainees did mention that they gained new knowledge and specific managerial skills for solving their specific managerial problems. However, such responses were few and far between.

A substantial number of trainees felt that they could not transfer their learning to the job as, immediately after training, they were given a new assignment unconnected with the training; or the training did not relate to the organisational conditions in which the trainee works. Another interesting finding of this study was that the bosses reported greater change in the trainees than what the trainees themselves reported. The trainees felt that they already knew what was taught. However, interviews with the bosses showed that though the trainees had the knowledge earlier, the training programme resulted in a greater consciousness which prompted them to bring about changes after training. Therefore, the bosses felt that the development of awareness was in itself an advantage of training. Similarly, the attitude of the bosses shows a favourable organisational climate towards changes as compared to what the trainees themselves reported. This again indicates some sort of a lack of communication between the bosses and the subordinates about training and its transfer. Where the bosses and the subordinates discussed an action plan for change, there was a greater transfer of learning and also greater support from the superiors for implementing changes.

To improve the effectiveness of training, it may be desirable to have a dovetailing of the objectives of the sponsoring organisation, the trainee, his superiors and the training institution. This can be achieved by:

1. The concerned parties meeting at periodic intervals.
2. The organisations having a clear three–five year growth plan, giving details of anticipated movements, both vertical and lateral. This will facilitate the setting of specific objectives for the training programme, specific standards for validation and also to plan the training strategies, and identification of training needs. This will also prompt the trainees and the trainers to undertake programmes for self-growth and thereby ensure the effectiveness of training. No doubt, there will be difficulties in achieving this. However, an attempt can be made to maximise the areas of agreement.
3. The objectives could be qualitative as well as quantitative. Organisations might have a specific number to be trained during a period. However, giving too much importance to the quantitative aspects can result in the qualitative objective being overlooked. The study also revealed that in many

cases, the managers themselves were not clear about the objectives of their jobs. Understanding the objectives of training can be a far-fetched expectation, given such situations. What is required is first to make job objective charts. However, where the training is based on whether or not people can be spared, then one cannot expect meaningful objectives for training.

4. Objectives for skill-oriented programmes can be clear and specific. However, for general management programmes, 'aimed at improvements in attitude, motivation, confidence, leadership and other behavioural dimensions', objectives will be mainly of a general nature, or, at times, they could be a combination of specific and general.

5. Matching of the training content to the objectives can be obtained by giving the training institutions all details of the trainees—biographical details, organisational background, level of maturity, expectations out of training (of the organisation as well as trainees)—well in advance so that the trainers can make suitable changes to the training inputs. This matching of objectives to the training content will be more difficult in the case of external training programmes. In fact, the major focus of training should be on internal training programmes; and the external training should supplement the internal efforts. At times, effort can also be made to internalise some of the external training programmes when a set of externally trained personnel is available.

6. It is imperative that the trainee be involved in the identification of his/her own training needs. The training aspects could also be linked to the annual appraisal report. However, care should be taken to see that such reporting is not perceived as a weakness and come in the way of the trainee's professional growth. A lot of sincere reporting will take place if this is assured. This, in turn, will help ensure the basic objective of training for improvement and growth. It may even be advisable to have a separate appraisal for developmental purposes, which should not be made available to those responsible for promotion decisions.

7. The attitude of the top management plays a pivotal role in making training more effective. The commitment of the higher administrative echelons to training and development can help smoothly merge training with other functions in the organisation.

The training institutions have a vital role to play in obtaining this commitment. This commitment of the top management can be obtained through:

1. Advisory boards which meet regularly and discuss issues pertaining to training and development;
2. Formal/informal sessions to bring out clearly the role of top level functionaries in training activity;
3. Involving the top level managers in inaugural, valedictory, and experience-sharing sessions;
4. Trainers should build up a rapport with the top management. This will be possible if the training section is headed by a very senior person and regularly informs the top decision-makers about training programmes, their contents, evaluation studies, and how training had led to improved performance; and
5. There should be training coordinators in each large department. These persons would be able to apprise the top management about training activities, assist in proper and adequate nominations and also facilitate evaluations.

The basic idea behind training is to improve the overall effectiveness and thereby reduce waste in the use of manpower, money and materials. The measurement of this improved effectiveness is the crux of any evaluation of training. Learning should be transferred to the job. The basic requirements to facilitate this transfer are:

1. A supportive organisational climate (systems have to be evolved for measuring such a climate);
2. Top level administrative/managerial commitment (barriers of hierarchy hinder actual transfer of learning and also make training difficult);

3. A high level of motivation among trainees;
4. The right attitude on the part of the trainer. If this is missing, it may lead to resistance towards learning; and
5. Consistency of views on the fundamental objectives among trainers.

In the ultimate analysis, it is the performance on-the-job that is the best measure of the effectiveness of training. Hence, a coordinated effort between the user organisations and the training institutions/trainers is very necessary in the evaluation of training in terms of its transfer to the job.

6

Management Education and Training in the Changing Environment

Over the last two decades, there has been a rapid growth in the number of institutions offering management education. The interdisciplinary nature of management education and its professional character differentiate it from a purely academic discipline. As a result, many public and private training institutions offer training courses in various fields of management. Management education, research and consulting have therefore been developed in the following categories of institutions.

1. *Educational Institutions* Universities offering degrees or diploma courses in management. This includes the Indian Institutes of Management.

2. *The National Institutes of Management* These institutions, such as the Administrative Staff College of India, Hyderabad, train practising managers and other executives in service.

3. *Private Management Institutions* Institutions with or without affiliation to universities, catering to particular fields of management such as the Xavier Labour Relations Institute.

4. *Discipline-based Institutes*   After independence, the need for a strong technological educational base was recognised and the Indian Institutes of Technology (IITs) were set up.

5. *Sectoral Institutes*   Specific industrial sectors have established their own management educational institutions like the National Institute of Banking Management and the Institute of Defence Management.

6. *Professional Institutes and Associations*   These are institutions which provide specialised professional education such as the Institute of Chartered Accountants, Institute of Cost and Works Accountants, Indian Society for Training and Development, National Institute of Personnel Management and All India Management Association.

7. *In-company Training Institutions*   Comprehensive in-company training institutions are a relatively recent phenomenon. Well-established private and public sector enterprises have incorporated the training activity catering to their own needs. Pioneers in the field are Hindustan Steel Ltd, Life Insurance Corporation of India, Ashok Leyland Ltd, State Trading Corporation, Bharat Heavy Electrical Ltd and Indian Oil Corporation.

8. *Management Trainee Schemes*   Many companies have their own management trainee schemes, recruiting young graduates for general and functional management training as part of their management development programmes.

Thus management education has grown rapidly to cover a number of sectors, disciplines and functions. Perhaps what should cause concern is the proliferation of such institutions in a manner that is not conducive to the sound development and effective utilisation of managerial resources.

Relevance of Management Education

The management education programmes offered by some of these institutions attempt to equip prospective managers to deal with organisational management and also to prepare them to shoulder higher responsibilities and improve their decision-making skills. Any advancement of management education requires appropriate human resource. This is linked to the development of an appropriate faculty which will play a leading role in inculcating the right managerial values and concepts among existing and future managers.

With the diversion of sizeable economic and human resources into this area, there should be a simultaneous endeavour to study the various factors that affect management education and training, right from identification of training needs, to the impact of management education on the efficiency of managers and its effect on the organisation.

But very little has been done to study the impact of management education and to improve management education from the point of view of the organisations. There has been little research to see whether and to what extent, these training institutions have succeeded in preparing managers to cope with their future responsibilities. With these objectives in mind, some pilot studies of a few organisations were undertaken to ascertain whether management education did result in organisational improvement through changed or different managerial behaviour. The preliminary findings indicate that students, in the initial years, perceived a gap between what was taught and what actually happens in the organisation. They found that there were too many pulls and pressures which did not gel with the management concepts taught in the institutes. It takes trainees quite a few years to understand the dynamics of the organisation, work out compromises and evolve their own style of management which is workable in the Indian context but is not necessarily in line with what they have been taught. Part of the problem also related to the fact that management concepts, borrowed from the West, were not applicable to the Indian value system.

This raises the issue of the relevance of education, especially when the global scenario is changing so fast that managerial obsolescence itself becomes an issue. The manager's world is more complex and less theoretical than any academic model. It is relatively easy to devise ideal teaching packages, but such packages cannot be absorbed unless they are:

1. Relevant to current needs;
2. Indicative of solutions to future problems; and
3. Grounded in managerial experience.

These constraints pose corresponding problems for management teaching and tend to eliminate teaching methods which

1. Do not take into account the environment of trainees in their work situation;
2. Are unable to interpret economic, technical, legal, political and social indicators; and
3. Are unable to take a managerial view of problems.

The third constraint mentioned above cannot be eased solely by the knowledge from Indian (or Western or Japanese) educational systems or by technical expertise or through managing someone or something. A combination of all three may help meet the requirement but this is rare.

Role of Management Development Teachers/Institutions

There is a lot of ambiguity with regard to the role of management development teachers and practitioners. Many describe their role humbly as sounding boards, facilitators, catalysts, providers of resources and, ultimately, the resources themselves. It is assumed that the management teacher or practitioner knows—or finds out from job descriptions and specifications—what knowledge, skills and attitudes a manager needs for his job, and sets out to inculcate these attitudes in the manager. In this case, the practitioner sees himself/herself as the controller of management development and the manager is developed as a passive product of the programme. In this approach, it is assumed that the teacher is taking a responsibility, based on his/her special expertise, for achieving something and setting out to achieve it. It has been agreed that management education has its impact through influencing attitudes as well as developing skills in getting things done. This raises the question about how individuals in occupational groupings, and managers in particular, come to have attitudes which are, to some degree, shared. This is called the 'socialisation process'. The important thing is to find out what role the management institutions and teachers can play in the socialising process. The important issue here is also how relevant the socialisation process is to the future needs of the manager. It is possible that institutions may be preparing 'past managers for past problems' or justifying 'current management practices' or teaching something which is irrelevant to the manager's world in the Indian context.

The aim of discussing all these aspects is to evaluate teaching methods, objectives and value systems in order to bring about changes to develop managers in real sense. Thus, management institutes must endeavour to acquire:

1. New techniques of aiding learning;
2. A new understanding of people in the system—and this can only be achieved through project or research-based work;
3. New knowledge of the work environment;
4. A new relationship between those who pay to learn and those who are paid to learn; and
5. A new approach to the whole question of relationship between life, work and the learning process.

It is interesting to see how our attitude to learning has changed over the last few years from the 'little learning is a dangerous thing' point of view, to the concept of whole organisation as a learning system.

Some of the relevant issues related to management education and organisations are:

1. Is education relevant to the needs of industry and business, or is it merely a source of information and a useful mental exercise which does not meet the organisation's present needs?

2. Do the training institutions offer management programmes because they can make a constructive contribution to management education, or are they unaware of the kind of impact they should make?
3. Do the organisations value management development and development of human resources as a matter of faith, as something that is right to do, a matter of prestige or is it merely a vague belief that some benefits are bound to accrue?

There is little research into the history of management knowledge and how it should be integrated into the Indian context. A large amount of effort has gone into evaluation research in the western countries. However, all such research is based on certain assumptions about how the practitioner brought about changes in the manager's knowledge, skills, and attitude and the consequences of these changes. Though these results are presumably intended to contribute to some grand theory of management, there is no sign of this even in advanced countries like the U.S. and the U.K.

Research and Management Education

It would, therefore, appear that the thrust of management development—especially the development of human resources—which can play a crucial role in the advancement of management education should be towards research, rather than purely teaching techniques. Some of the areas of research could be:

1. *How Managers Learn* The question of what a manager learns and how he/she learns it is essential to the development of management education. An important value judgement is implied here: Should management teaching be directed primarily towards the needs of the organisation or towards those of the individuals? There is also the issue of off-the-job teaching or on-the-job teaching. We ought to understand how far managers are influenced by the teaching of their superiors and, if it is to a great

extent then we ought to simultaneously improve the manager's teaching and learning apparatus.

2. *How the Transfer of Learning is Affected* The current dis-enchantment of management teachers with business games as a medium for acquiring decision-making knowledge is based upon the criticism that it only teaches managers how to play business games by being bold and risky, when industry requires logical, cautious, risk-minimising, managers. Besides, we also need to consider the knowledge that is imparted. Does a manager manage better by being able to write a computer programme or operate a nation state? What are the managerial skills that he/she could be taught to perform that will improve his/her contribution to the firm? What is the optimum balance of theory and practice in the teaching activity and how can it be achieved? In any case, research into the transfer of learning can cover such matters as: the use of projects, the creation of case studies derived from the 'home' organisations, the study of the organisational environ-ment, and the investigation of the nature of the social contract between the manager and his/her firm.

3. *Transfer of Managerial Technology from Foreign Countries to the Indian Setting* The problems arising out of the transfer of managerial technology from western countries to Indian condi-tions is an important issue. However, in order to yield positive results, the imported management curriculum must be modified to suit Indian conditions. The content should be designed to ulti-mately result in a change of management behaviour. It has been realised that many of the conceptual schemes and managerial practices, which form the substance of management education, were evolved in industrial countries. When they are imported into a developing country, they often are in direct conflict with the traditional values. This creates barriers which interfere with the learning process.

Research work done by Virmani and Guptan in India, G. Redding at the University of Hong Kong, and by Paul Streeton in England in the transfer of intellectual, social, economic and managerial technology from the advanced to the developing countries are pointers towards the need to evolve methods appropriate to the local culture rather than trying to apply foreign techniques indiscriminately.

4. *Skills and Demands of Managerial Jobs and Roles*   There are hardly any studies in India on managerial behaviour, partly due to the lack of effective monitoring devices. Real behaviour is what counts. However, at the moment, we can only guess at the difference in what the managers say they are/do, and what they really are/do. An interesting fact noticed during the author's study on management trainee schemes in Indian organisations was the large gap between the managers' perception of the trainees' attitudes towards their training programme and their job-satisfaction, and the trainees' own attitude. The managers perceived their trainees to have more positive attitudes towards their training scheme than trainees themselves do; and this perceived gap resulted in a high turnover. This equips us with a better idea of how we ought to teach future managers in different professions or environments.

5. *Perception Gap between Managers' Needs and Training Needs* There has also been found to be a gap not only between what managers say they do and what they think they ought to do but also between how they perceive the needs of the organisation and the actual educational needs for successful management. These might arise due to the conflict between the personal needs of managers and the organisational needs thus posing a problem in identifying the actual teaching needs.

6. *Management Institutions and Educational Needs*   To successfully identify the actual needs of the manager, the teachers of management need to critically analyse and distinguish between those types of training which the manager can see to be immediately relevant and those which may be relevant in the future. The teacher must be able to distinguish between what can be done in

the classroom at work; what can be done in the classroom away from work; and what cannot be done in the classroom at all. The teacher should also be aware of what the organisation wants for the managers and what the managers want for themselves so that a policy, which embraces both sorts of training, on management development packages is formulated.

7. *Managerial Effectiveness*   Once again, little is known about the ways in which ineffective managers can become effective (by challenge, opportunity or experience) and effective managers become ineffective (by promotion, transfer, obsolescence or old age). If we are to seek improved managerial effectiveness, we should create an atmosphere which rewards the effective manager while simultaneously encouraging the ineffective one. This, however, has design implications that may move towards conformism; and it also poses the problem of evaluation which will then become a behavioural criterion rather than one of raising morale or knowledge absorption.

Conclusion

For the advancement of management education in India, it is important to see how the persons connected with management education and management institutions fully understand the Indian environment, the organisational problems and the global scenario. This calls for an initial focus on research for the development of the human resources connected with the management education. Some of the major areas of research can be:

1. Research into the nature of the manager's selection: what are the criteria for selection for management development programmes and how far should on-the-job performance (or the lack of it) affect the design of development programmes? Research in this area should centre around the function of the organisation in arranging for suitable management development, and will provide answers to questions

such as how much pre-course conditioning (reading, questionnaires, seminars) is possible or desirable.

2. Research to investigate not only techniques, but also questions of pace, timing, priorities and feedback, to test the relative importance of individual and group learning. We need to quantify success and failure for teachers and students and relate these to a number of variables.

3. Research to determine the relevance of the teaching material to managerial requirements. Despite attempts to professionalise management teaching, a large number of the traditionally managed Indian organisations still do not insist upon minimum managerial qualifications. Countries like Japan and Germany did not have business management schools till recently and still these countries advanced tremendously. This gives an indication that there is a need for the improvement of evaluation systems for management education.

4. Research in the area of transfer of managerial technology from advanced to developing countries. We should undertake some research study to determine the appropriateness of the western or Japanese managerial technology based on cultural beliefs and value systems prevailing in India.

In the fast changing national and international environment, there could be a grave danger that those connected with management education become outdated rapidly. Therefore, there is a tremendous need to have adequate updated information, storage and retrieval systems to cull out relevant information from a plethora of data that is published daily. Frankly speaking, how many of us have the time to read and do basic research in our Indian context, when the rewards come from quick consulting, delivering short papers and talks, and playing 'professional games'? All these activities are taking more time and could detract from our most basic responsibility of research and research-based teaching and consultancy. As a result, there can be a danger of being perceived not as the fountainheads of change and creative education, but as warehouses of the 'latest fads' in management education.

References

1. **Redding, G.** and **Casey, T.**, 'Managerial Beliefs among Asian Managers', *Proceedings of the Academy of Management, 36th Annual Meeting*, Kansas City 1976.
2. **Schein, Edgar H.**, 'Organisational Socialisation in the Early Career of Industrial Managers'. Paper presented at meetings of the New England Psychological Association, Massachusetts Institute of Technology, 8 November, 1963.
3. **Streeton, Paul,** 'The Limits of Development Research', *World Development*, Vol. 2, No. 10–12, pp. 11–34, October–December 1974.
4. **Virmani, B.R.** and **Seth, Premila,** *Evaluating Management Training and Development*, Vision Books, New Delhi, 1985.
5. **Virmani, B.R.,** *Management Training and Development—An Evaluation Approach,* Indian Society for Training and Development, New Delhi, 1998.
6. **Virmani, B.R.** and **Guptan, Sunil Unny,** *Indian Management*, Vision Books, New Delhi, 1991.
7. **Virmani, B.R.** and **Rao, Kala,** *Economic Restructuring, Technology Transfer and Human Resource Development*, Second Edition, Response Books, Sage Publications, New Delhi, 1999.

7

Developing Technical Training Schemes

Increasing the skills and capabilities of employees is the key to economic success in an increasingly integrated and competitive global economy. Investing in people can boost the living standards by expanding opportunities, raising productivity, attracting capital investment and increasing earning power. The importance of technical training is of utmost significance for any fast developing economy.

With the increasing liberalisation of the economy, improvements in productivity are not possible without adopting the latest technology. Proper engineering education and training are essential for this. The author, in association with the Federation of Indian Chambers of Commerce and Industry (FICCI), undertook a study of the problem of engineer trainees in various organisations. This covered 90 organisations and a representative sample of over 30 technical training institutions including the Indian Institutes of Technology (IITs) and Regional Engineering Colleges (RECs). The data was collected through questionnaires, personal interviews of engineers and the faculty of engineering colleges and institutes as well as discussions with government officials dealing with apprenticeship schemes. This chapter highlights some of the major findings of the study and some general suggestions to improve the engineer trainee schemes.

Industry and Educational Institutes

The industry and the engineering institutions have misgivings about each other's roles. Industry feels that engineering institutions are not in tune with their needs while the engineering colleges complain of lack of co-operation from industry. The major areas of discontent relate to curriculum design, interaction between industry and the engineering colleges, haphazard in-plant training, poor facilities for practical training in the colleges, ineffective training during apprenticeship and lack of interest in government apprenticeship schemes. The industry complained that training institutions were reluctant to involve their faculty in the problems of industry.

Salient Features of Training during Apprenticeship Period in Industry

Most of the large industries prefer to have their own graduate engineer trainee schemes rather than rely upon the statutory apprenticeship scheme. Where there are trainees from both schemes, they are treated differently. More attention is paid to one's own trainees while the apprentices under statutory schemes are treated more as a liability than an asset.

However, there is frustration among the graduate engineers under both schemes. The main dissatisfaction comes from a lack of meaningful responsibility during the initial years of training. Where responsibility was given, the engineers turned out to be better later on and the turnover was also less. Where the training was elaborate, consisting of job rotation, project work and lectures, the frustration was greater. The trainees complained of a lack of interest on the part of the top management and their senior managers.

The training officers in charge of engineer trainees were them-selves dissatisfied with the training programmes and their role and status in the organisations. They felt that the training cell does not offer better prospects. Therefore, they had no commit-ment to training, further adding to their frustration.

There were lacunae in the system of appraisal of graduate engin-eers during the training period. It was subjective, personality-oriented and was not used for personnel development.

There was a lack of proper career planning and the progress of most of the engineers was erratic. Some progressed quickly, others slowly. The progress was not directly connected to their performance but related to extraneous factors like being placed in a department which offered quick prospects.

There was a perception gap between the management and the trainees regarding the reasons for the turnover of trainees during training itself. The common reasons for turnover cited by the top management are higher salary, better career prospects, better location, and other personal reasons. On the other hand, the reasons given by the engineer trainees themselves were defective training programmes, lack of challenging assignments in the ini-tial years, non-acceptability of graduate engineer trainee schemes by senior engineers, long and purposeless induction period, in-adequate career planning, indifferent selection procedure and unsuitable corporate climate.

The young engineers, specially from IITs prefer management positions or design jobs in the head office, with the result that industry feels that engineers from good institutions are not pre-pared to work at shop-floor level engineering positions. Industry also complained about the lack of knowledge on the part of the engineers of some of the administrative aspects of the engineer-ing functions.

Training of Engineers in Engineering Colleges

There were variations in the duration of engineering education. While most institutes have four-year programmes, some have a five-year programme for a bachelor of engineering (BE) degree. The ratio of students to faculty varies from 10 to 20. In some institutions the ratio varies from 10 to 40. This problem is more acute in the area of civil and electrical engineering. It was also felt that barring a few institutions, good engineers do not prefer to go in for teaching careers due to lack of incentives.

Most engineering colleges are not satisfied with their own workshop, laboratory and library facilities. There is no repair, maintenance or modernisation of these facilities. The reasons for this are lack of finance and appropriate planning.

All the colleges indicated the need for a periodic revision of the curriculum to keep pace with the changes in technology. However, a substantial number of engineering colleges had changed their curriculum only once (or in some cases twice) in the last 10 years. The standardisation of engineering curriculum for all colleges was not favoured. It was felt that certain colleges meet research needs while others meet the requirements of the shop-floor. Moreover, it was felt that standardisation of curriculum will not help standardise the quality of the student; this will depend upon the quality of teachers and the infrastructure facilities available in different colleges.

Most engineering colleges were dissatisfied with the quality of practical training. This was said to be primarily due to lack of appropriate co-operation from industry. It was suggested that government should make a mandatory provision that all industries accept students for training for a fixed period. The sandwich courses offered by some technical institutes were considered more relevant and should be extended to other colleges.

There was little interaction between the training institutions and industry, and even this was confined to making arrangements for in-plant training for students or the selection of engineers by the industry. There was no meaningful interaction in order to get acquainted with the changing requirements of industry.

There was a perception gap about the kind of training to be given to engineers. The colleges felt that they should concentrate on giving a good foundation in engineering and the industry should take up the role of preparing engineers for specific jobs.

The industry, on the other hand, expects the students passing out of these colleges to be ready for the jobs they are selected for. But even if the institutes prepare engineers for a specific job, there is no likelihood that they will readily get that job. Some faculty members, especially from the IITs, felt that the IITs have been concentrating lot on extremely advanced industrial technology. This, at times, leads to frustration not only among engineers but in industry also, because both realised there was a gap between the technologies the engineers were trained for and the technologies that exist in the workplace.

Hurdles in the Way of Effective Technical Training

1. *Problems of Interface between Teaching Institutions and Industry*
Teaching institutions try to encourage their faculty to take up assignments related to basic research and consultancy. However, a number of projects get dropped midway or result in short papers. Most of the projects are not relevant to industry. The industry prefers to import ready-made processes from abroad. There is also a paucity of funds for research and a lack of interest on the part of industry for any research.

2. *Engineering Curriculum and Management Education*   Most of the engineers prefer to take up management positions instead of engineering positions because of the better salary and career prospects. Many engineering colleges plan to start full-time management courses and, in fact, encourage their engineers to go in for these. Industry as well as some faculty members frown on this as they feel that this encourages engineers to go in for management positions. On the contrary, they recommend that some management subjects like costing, personnel and labour laws and marketing be integrated into the engineering curriculum.

3. *Engineers and the Jobs They Take Up*   There was an extreme mismatch between the interest, background and specialisation of the engineers and the jobs they take up. For example, an electronic

engineer may have a job in maintenance. Placement was more related to employment factors rather than the interest or aptitude of engineers. This was found to be one of the major factors for discontentment and high turnover among engineers reflecting on the faulty planning of recruitment policies.

4. *Statutory Apprenticeship Scheme* The statutory apprenticeship scheme was not favoured either by industry, or engineering colleges or the engineers themselves. They felt that only inferior students normally go in for the statutory scheme. Therefore, everyone felt that this needs to be abolished and substituted with a more pragmatic and useful scheme.

Overcoming the Hurdles

Some suggestions and recommendations have been made to overcome these hurdles and pave the way for effective technical training.

Suggestions for the Engineering Colleges

There is a need for greater interaction between the engineering colleges and the industry. This can be done only if more applied research projects are taken up on behalf of the industry. The faculty of the colleges should not limit themselves to basic research or to publication of papers without bothering about their applicability to industry. Interaction could also improve if faculty members work in industry for fixed periods instead of just study tours of a month or two.

It is not desirable to standardise the curriculum of all the engineering colleges. Different institutions meet different needs. Therefore, there should be some very broad guidelines and the specific curriculum should be developed internally. There is also a need to revise the curriculum periodically to keep pace with the changing needs of technology and industry. There is a need to streamline the practical training given during a graduate course. Instead of sending students for practical training for periods ranging from 15 days to a month, it may be worthwhile having a block placement of six months in a particular organisation where a student is asked to work on a project and prepare the report.

There is need to have appropriate maintenance, budgeting and planning for the institution's workshop, laboratory and library. The salary structure and other incentives for the engineering faculty need to be improved to attract the best talent. The faculty–student ratio should be maintained at 1:10.

It is not possible for engineering colleges to prepare students for specific jobs in industry. They must concentrate on good general engineering education; and the industry should prepare engineers for specific jobs through their own apprenticeship schemes. The colleges should see that the technology is relevant in the immediate Indian context; they should not use obsolete technology or highly advanced technology which is far ahead of its time.

Suggestions for Industry

The engineer trainee schemes need streamlining, based on appropriate manpower and career planning (both short-term and long-term) within the organisation.

Internal training should be divided into three parts:

1. Induction training;
2. Specialised training schemes for engineers who have to be developed in specialised skills required for a particular job or function; and
3. Continuing education and training to prepare engineers for new tasks based on changing technology.

The recruitment policy of the graduate engineer trainees needs to be modified to ensure that jobs are given to the engineers in line with their interests. The training programme also needs to be streamlined. It may be worthwhile to give graduate engineer trainees responsible tasks after a brief induction period rather than putting them through a long induction programme of one or two years' duration. The accent should be on learning while doing rather than pure theoretical learning. The post of training officers or instructors should not be treated as a dumping ground for inefficient engineers. Their status and position need improvement.

There is a need for better communication between the engineering trainees and the top management so that they are able to understand each other's problems.

The industry should discourage engineers, especially those from the IITs, to be taken straight for design jobs. They should start with shop-floor positions and then be gradually trained and developed for design and other jobs in line with their interests. The appraisal systems of the graduate engineer trainees need streamlining and should be used primarily for developmental purposes.

The recruitment of engineers directly to managerial positions in non-engineering functions should be discouraged. The salary structure of engineers should be brought on par with other non-engineering executives/managerial positions. This will discourage engineers from going in for managerial positions.

As far as possible, the industries should involve the faculty of the engineering colleges in developing new processes and technology rather than merely importing technology.

Some General Recommendations

Instead of engineering colleges starting their own management courses, it will be more useful if managerial and administrative aspects of the engineering function are made a part of the engineering curriculum.

The statutory apprenticeship schemes for graduate engineers should be abolished. Instead, it should be made obligatory for industry to accept a certain number of engineering students for a block practical training placement for at least six months. During this period, the trainees will work on specific projects that will then be evaluated by the engineering colleges; they should be declared eligible for final degree only after the successful completion of this training.

This interface between teaching institutions and industry should be encouraged. There should be exchange of personnel between the two, for long durations, to work on specific assignments/projects.

8

Workers' Education:
Perspectives for Future Action

Workers' education in India centres around the Central Board for Workers' Education (CBWE) established in 1958 as a semi-autonomous body under the ministry of labour. The Board has about 50 regional centres spread all over India and also runs the Indian Institute of Workers' Education at Bombay. The CBWE programme uses three levels of training. At the first level, education officers, who are top-level training officers are trained in the Indian Institute of Workers' Education. When they complete their training, they are assigned to the regional centres. In the second level, these officers train selected worker-teachers in groups of 25–30 in full-time courses of three months' duration each. Worker-teacher trainees are normally sponsored either by the trade unions or by the management. Finally, on completion of their training, the worker-teachers return to their establishments and conduct programmes for workers in their workplace.

By the end of 1994, the CBWE claims to have trained over five million workers under different categories including worker-teachers and workers, both at unit-level classes and by the grantees (i.e., trade unions which receive monetary grants from CBWE to conduct their own workers' education classes).

Objectives and Contents

The initial objectives of Indian worker education, stated by the government, were as follows:

1. To develop stronger and more effective unions through better-trained officials and more enlightened members;
2. To develop leadership from the rank and file and promote the growth of democratic processes and traditions in unions;
3. To equip organised labour to effectively fulfil its social and economic responsibilities and take its place in a democratic society; and
4. To promote a greater understanding among workers of the problems of their economic environment and their privileges and obligations as union members, officials and citizens.

On the basis of recommendations of the G. Ramanujam Committee which reviewed the status of workers' education in 1974–75, the CBWE's objectives placed greater emphasis on labour's involvement in economic development, the obligations and responsibilities of workers, and on the development of 'responsible' trade unions. It was also decided that the CBWE should concentrate more on the education of rural workers; the responsibility of educating industrial workers should be shifted to the trade unions, which will receive grants for this purpose.

The main topics to be covered in the training programme are: the purpose of unions, union organisation and administration, union-management relations, unions and national development, general safety and family welfare, collective bargaining, financial aspects of industry, labour productivity, participative management, workers' rights and obligations, discipline, labour legislation, work organisation, wage systems, rationalisation and technology, labour economics and socio-political environment. In addition, the worker-teachers are also taught training methods and techniques.

In addition to the CBWE, there are adult literacy programmes conducted under the auspices of the National Adult Education Programme. Institutions such as the ASCI, National Labour Institute (NLI), and Institute for Miners' and Metalworkers' Education also have occasional training activities. Finally, some unions and certain large organisations like the International Confederation of Free Trade Unions (ICFTU) have workers' education schemes of their own.

Evaluation of Workers' Education

Workers' education has been subject to periodic evaluation. The CBWE's own studies are typically superficial and often termed 'white-wash'; they find nothing wrong and generally conclude that there has been a positive effect of workers' education. But other studies give a different picture. For example, the National Commission on Labour (1967) and the Ramanujam Committee reported that the programme had little impact and that much more needs to be done. It was with this background that a detailed study of workers' education schemes in India was undertaken. The study revealed a number of basic problems that need to be resolved before workers' education can have any meaningful impact.

Evaluation Methodologies

Before presenting the main findings, it may be appropriate to describe the methodology of the study.

The earlier studies were based on questionnaires, formal interviews, and what government committees call 'evidence'. The author and his team used questionnaires and formal interviews at first. Later on, however, when they switched to informal discussions with rank and file workers, they got some very different opinions. A number of respondents—some union leaders, management functionaries and even CBWE functionaries—declined to fill out formal questionnaires but were willing to speak to informally, provided they were not named or quoted. Many of their comments were inconsistent with the formal opinions reported in earlier studies. Consequently, the study team decided to interview informally even those who had answered the formal questionnaires. Once again, the views expressed informally contradicted those expressed in writing.

For example, the formal position taken by most parties was that unions should take over the responsibility for workers' education. But during informal discussions, there was almost unanimous agreement (including among some top union leaders) that unions were just not prepared to do this. Trade unions were victims of the personality cult, politicised and were busy fighting with each other. Therefore, funds given to them for workers' education may get misused.

Similar differences between formal and off-the-record positions were evident regarding such issues as course content, selection of workers for training, and conduct of the unit level classes. These variations occur because all decisions with regard to workers' education are highly centralised, whether in the government, trade unions or the CBWE itself. As a consequence, subordinates have little freedom to express their own views. Also, many of the formal objectives of workers' education, though morally and ethically desirable, are inconsistent with the real interests of managements, trade unions or the government. Therefore, a frank expression of views may lead to reprisals.

Many policy decisions are based on formal studies but the ground reality may be very different. The result is that policy decisions are difficult to implement. This is exactly what has happened with regard to workers' education. Most of the earlier studies either ignored, or paid little attention to, the opinions of the workers in designing the curriculum. The author's study was based on intensive, informal discussions with people at all levels, including those at the very bottom. With this methodological introduction, let us summarise the findings.

Programme Implementation

1. The top management in almost all the organisations is either indifferent to or ignorant about the workers' education scheme. It is mostly delegated to junior or insignificant officers in the organisation who do not have much of a say in matters.
2. The middle-level managements, both in the private and public sectors, are either indifferent or unwilling to go along with the scheme, unless it covers those subjects that are of interest to the management. Interestingly, though the workers' education scheme is a government programme, greater indifference is found in government organisations.
3. Wherever the managements have taken an active interest, the scheme worked. However, when it was left to the trade unions, it became an issue for rivalries within and between unions and for union-management confrontations.
4. Both unions and managements have reservations about the content of the curriculum. Each sees it as being biased against them and none of the involved parties feel that workers' education has achieved its stated objectives.
5. The all-India tour, as part of the training programmes, is considered to be the major attraction of the workers' education scheme. Among the main motivations for attending classes were the various holidays and incentives—including a break from regular work. As a consequence, workers have little incentive for any real learning.
6. Worker-teachers perceive the scheme as a ticket for holding union office and not for training workers. In fact, only a minority of the worker-teachers conduct the regular unit-level classes for which they are trained. The main reason for not conducting classes is attributed to lack of management and/or trade union support, lack of incentives, inter-union rivalries, and incompetence of the worker-teachers due to their faulty selection.
7. The scheme envisages a three-tier system of training education officers, worker-teachers and unit level workers; how-

ever its impact at the unit level was ineffective. There was a lot of demoralisation among the CBWE staff, especially the education officers, in terms of their salaries, career advancement and recruitment of education officers. There was too much of centralisation at the CBWE; very little freedom was given to the regional level units, even to take routine decisions. There was a lack of upward communication and the regional units were expected to follow and defend the decisions taken at the central level. There were no opportunities for the education officers to develop themselves; but at the same time they were expected to teach all the major subjects, which they found impossible. The CBWE is now shifting emphasis to the education of workers in the rural and unorganised sector, expecting the trade unions to take over the responsibility of training industrial workers. This has been done without adequate preparation or reorientation of education officers; as a result, justice could be done to neither. In fact, the education of industrial workers has further deteriorated.

There are two views regarding the desirability of trade unions taking over workers' education. The minority view is that it is the trade union that can effectively educate its members and, therefore, it must set aside some funds for educational purposes. The majority view, however, is that Indian trade unions are financially weak, and if they are given funds they may misappropriate them. Also, given the multiplicity of unions, this will only generate rivalries.

Interestingly, few workers favour the government taking over workers' education. They feel that the government has a vested interest, being involved either as an employer or having a trade union affiliated to the political party in power. It was felt that no external political trade union leader will encourage teaching and the development of internal leadership from the rank and file. Respondents concluded that a totally independent body should be created to handle workers' education.

Syllabus

Most workers feel that the syllabus designed by the CBWE does not meet the stated objectives of the workers' education scheme. On the one hand, it emphasises that workers should be taught the moral philosophy of co-operation and be 'good'; on the other hand, the system followed in the organisation is that of crude, militant, collective bargaining and class conflict. Therefore, the workers see a wide gap between what is taught and what is practised, and this contradiction confuses them and makes them cynical. They lose faith in the process and content of education itself, and become demotivated and disinterested in the entire training process.

There are quite a few examples of the somewhat hypocritical nature of the formal syllabus. One of the programme's main objectives is to develop rank-and-file leadership. However, nothing is said about the adverse effects on the union of having officers who are 'outsiders' and have not worked their way up through the ranks. Indeed, many workers feel that trade unions have little interest in developing internal leadership. Examples are cited of unions that have not conducted elections or changed leaders for years.

Similarly, another objective is to build strong, united and more responsible unions, but nowhere is it stated what being 'strong' or 'responsible' means. Most workers believe that their union should be responsible to its members and that it should not come into the picture where their individual performance was concerned. But the syllabus is unclear as to whom the workers should be responsible to—the unions, company or the government. All have conflicting interests.

The formal syllabus is also inconsistent with what is actually taught. In part, this was because no single education officer or worker-teacher was capable of teaching all the complicated subjects the syllabus prescribed, and in part it was because some of the topics were threatening either to the management or the union leadership. Thus, areas of controversy were downplayed and safe subjects, such as Indian history and culture, received more attention. Workers felt that such subjects did not help in improving their skills or attitude.

The selection procedure for worker-teachers came under heavy criticism. It was felt that worker-teachers were rarely selected on the basis of their teaching ability. Barring some exceptions, politics influenced their selection. When left to the unions, the main selection criterion was personal loyalty to the leaders; when left to the management, it was loyalty to the management. When both were involved, it became an issue for collective bargaining, which, in many cases, resulted in the whole education scheme being dropped.

The interview data showed that the preferred selection criteria should include:

1. Attendance at unit-level classes;
2. Minimum educational qualifications;
3. Capacity and level of expression; and
4. Ability, aptitude and commitment to take unit-level classes.

There must be rigid screening by an independent body. It was also suggested that education officers should specialise, with each one teaching part of the curriculum.

Though on paper it was said that 'new directions' and 'new dimensions' were given to the workers' education scheme, very little has changed in reality. In the curriculum, greater emphasis was supposed to have been given on developing responsible trade unionism, the development of internal leadership, obligations of workers; in reality, the same subjects were taught without much change. Though the syllabus was supposed to be prepared by a tripartite committee, there are many instances where the members of the committee were not even aware of the total scheme or the curriculum. What is worse, some of them did not attend most of the committee meetings.

Impact of Workers' Education

In the management's view, workers' education has had relatively little impact. There is fear that it encourages union rivalry. It is also felt that after training, workers sometimes become more militant regarding their rights, thus leading to strains in the union–management relationship.

Union leaders were divided in their views. Where unions had the exclusive right to nominate workers for training, they felt training helped build internal leadership. But where other selection criteria were used, unions feared that workers' education had the adverse effect of making workers disloyal to their unions.

Significantly, the workers' own views about the benefits of training differed widely. The majority reported that it had no effect at all; others felt it made them independent of the unions and the management, both of whom were seen as having a vested interest. In some cases, therefore, workers' education caused conflict with either the management or the union.

Four prerequisites should be met if workers are to grow personally and professionally. These are:

1. Better schooling and education;
2. Labour conditions which encourage the exercise of responsibility;
3. Security of minimum subsistence; and, only then
4. A continuing education so that the participants learn to courageously develop a sense of self-worth.

Going by this, the Indian situation is hardly conducive to effective workers' education. The schooling system discourages participation and encourages conformity. The management distrusts workers and is unwilling to share information or responsibility. Unions are fragmented, personality-oriented and interested mainly in politics. In fact, at times, workers distrust their union leaders as much as they do the management. Understandably, therefore, workers' education receives low priority. Though the schemes exist on paper, our study reveals they are little more than window-dressing.

Perspectives for Future Action

Keeping in view some of the study's findings, it may be worthwhile to restructure the workers' education scheme in a modular form. This should be designed to help workers and trade unionists progress from the basic to the intermediate level courses so that they can broaden their perceptions and develop their skills before proceeding to advanced level courses aimed at leadership training. Only those trainees showing promise should be allowed to move from the basic courses to the higher level courses.

Objectives

The proposed objectives of the scheme could be:

1. Improve literacy and remove ignorance;
2. Make the workers/trade unions conscious of their role in the country's development;
3. Develop a democratic, independent and strong trade union movement devoted to the workers' cause, free from day-to-day political interference;
4. Prepare workers to participate effectively in the decision-making process of the enterprise;
5. Check the abuse of power by the employers, trade union leaders and government functionaries through a healthy workers' movement;
6. Make the workers conscious of their rights as well as obligations towards their fellow workers and society as a whole; and
7. Change and broaden one's outlook on life.

It is often suggested that the multiplicity of institutions at various levels be ended. Instead there should be an autonomous institution at the national, regional and local levels which will be managed by a professional board. The national level board should formulate policies on the framework of workers' education, research, finances, and will exercise overall supervision over the regional institutes. The regional institutes can be set up in four or more regions. The local centres will be the real hubs of the workers' education scheme at the unit level. It will not only conduct education programmes but also combine training with recreation through study circles.

The main functions of these institutes could be:

1. *National Institute*   It will have the following major activities:

(a) Organising national-level training programmes for workers and senior trade union leaders, as well as workers' trainers. They will have a full-fledged research wing concentrating on issues connected with workers' education, and other general matters such as (i) collection of the cost of living index; (ii) average pattern of working conditions and wages in different industries; (iii) composition of the workforce; (iv) relations between development plans and labour; (v) workers' productivity; (vi) participative management; (vii) adult learning; (viii) evaluation of training programmes; and (xi) rationalisation and its impact.

(b) Disseminate the information so collected through regular publication of a journal.

(c) Publication of a journal and books and pamphlets on different aspects of workers' education, including training manuals, reading material and cases for training programmes at various levels.

2. *Regional Institutes*   These institutes will organise:

(a) Intermediate level training programmes for workers and trade union leaders in English as well as regional languages.

(b) Research and data collection on regional issues of workers' interest.

(c) Publication of reading material and books in different regional languages.

3. *Local Centres*   The local centres will have the following activities:

(a) Training programmes for rank and file workers.

(b) Adult literacy classes to be conducted in the evenings or during weekends.

(c) Provide a forum and reading material for discussion groups and study circles.

(d) Translating and disseminating materials in the local language.

(e) Publication of newsletters in the local language.

(f) Giving day-to-day data of interest to workers.

(g) Maintaining a library for workers.

4. *Study Circles*   The circles will hold periodic evening or weekend discussions at the local centre with the help of instructors. The centre will initially take the lead in organising such study circles with the help of the local trade unions and industries. The centre will also provide the study material and educational aids. Special reading material will have to be designed for use in the study circles. Initially there should be specialised training programmes for study circle leaders. They must be trained in conducting meetings, preparing reports, instruction methods, etc. The advantage of study circles is that they will be less expensive and cover a large number of workers. The study circles can identify potential participants for higher level training programmes. To sustain interest in the study circles, they should also have some recreational activities. As far as possible, all the workers must be covered under the study circles scheme and these could become the basic units of workers' education. The initial focus should be to identify and train leaders of the study circles. They should be able to help in conducting adult literacy classes. The instructors or education officers of the local centres will have to give a lot of help to the study circles in terms of providing physical facilities, reading material and some lectures on specialised topics. All the courses conducted by the local centres should be in the local language as far as possible.

5. *Correspondence Courses*   The national institute can also develop correspondence courses in general and functional subjects for various categories of workers, committee and council members and trade union leaders. Some of these courses can be in regional languages to be administered through regional institutes and local centres. These courses can be supplemented through periodic lectures at the local centres.

Training for Participative Management

All state governments have accepted the need for employee participation in management. Many research studies have indicated that there is a positive correlation between the level of education and participation in management activities.

A separate cell on participative management can be set up within the overall guidance of the national institute. The activities of this cell, to be headed by a director, can be divided into three parts: (a) conducting of training programmes for various levels of employees, from the workers to the managers, on participative management; (b) rendering advice and consultancy to employee representatives on participative councils and committees; and (c) conducting research and compiling data on the functioning and effectiveness of workers' participation in management, and publishing it in various languages.

Financial Resources for Institutes and Training Programmes

Grants should be arranged from the central government for the national institute, and from the state governments for the regional institutes. The local centres must be financed by the local industries. The fee for the workers attending the courses can be paid by the employers and/or the trade unions nominating their leaders/members for the courses. In this case they can pay a subsidised fee. The government can consider levying a 'cess' on all companies to contribute for the workers' education institute and this can be a deductible expense for tax purposes. Research and training grants can also be made available from national and international bodies like the Indian Council of Social Science Research, International Labour Organisation, Friedrich Ebert Foundation of Germany, Ford Foundation and International Trade Union Federations.

Facilities and Incentives for Training

There is a need for a law compelling organisations to release committee members, leaders of the recognised trade unions and workers for at least one to three weeks a year for training. This period should be treated as duty leave. The trainees will receive full pay and all the travelling and incidental expenses will be paid by the organisation.

Conclusion

The suggested proposal on workers' education may appear comprehensive and of an advanced level. There is a plethora of institutes dealing with workers' education. However, their impact has been marginal. The suggestions given will bring them together and ensure a better focus on workers' education. Workers have to be taken step by step from adult literacy classes to advanced level training. Any short-cuts will limit the impact of training and reduce workers' interest. Also, only professionals should run the scheme.

In India, there is already a tradition of tripartism in labour-management relations. A fully autonomous board comprising the government, employers and trade unions along with academicians should manage the proposed institute. The selection of the board need not be on the basis of only sectoral representation but also on their demonstrated interest in workers' education. In due course, it should become an autonomous board managed by professionals only. It is expected that the directors of the institute must be academicians acquainted with the problems of adult education and training. Research and publication activities must be undertaken in all the languages. This has been the Achilles' heel of the present scheme. Hopefully, the creation of a separate research cell will enhance these efforts. A national-level committee must be constituted to study the details of the proposed model and its implementation strategy. What is proposed here is only a tentative model; the proposed committee can work out the details and implementation strategy.

This chapter is confined to the issues connected with general education and training of workers. Skill development and technical training have been handled in a separate chapter.

References

1. **Ramaswamy, E.A.**, 'What Education do Workers Need?' in Virmani, B.R. and Hayder, U. (eds.): *Education, Training and Research for Employees' Participation in Management: Proceedings of an Indo-German Seminar,* 11–13 October 1982, Administrative Staff College of India, Hyderabad, pp. 155–77, 1984.
2. **Ramaswamy, U.**, *Work, Union and Community—Industrial Man in South India,* Oxford University Press, Delhi, 1983.
3. **Schneider, P.W.**, 'Workers Education in Germany' in Virmani, B.R. and Hayder, U. (eds.), see n. 1, pp. 89–110.
4. **Virmani, B.R.**, *Workers' Education in India,* Administrative Staff College of India and Friedrich Ebert Foundation, Hyderabad and Bonn, 1986.
5. **Virmani, B.R.** and **Klaus, J. Voll,** *Workers' Education,* Vision Books, New Delhi, 1989.
6. **Virmani, B.R.**, 'Redefining Industrial Relations', *Indian Journal of Industrial Relations,* Vol. 31, No. 2, Shri Ram Centre for Industrial Relations and Human Resources, pp. 153–77, October 1995.

9

Globalisation, Technological Changes and Human Resource Management

The economic development of a country depends on two important factors. One is the level of industrial development and the other is the economic, social and political environment. During the last decade, the world has seen major economic changes. Paradoxically, more and more regional trade blocs are being formed, and with the signing of the GATT and the formation of the World Trade Organisation (WTO) recently, some of the trade barriers are being reduced or eliminated. This has also created cut-throat competition among countries. In this restructuring process, technology is playing a crucial role. The need for continuous innovation, especially in high-tech industries, and the policies of various countries help to bring in sophisticated technology, and increase the product range in order to tap new markets and meet competition.

Globalisation

Till the late 1950s the world economy was divided into a number of loosely integrated groups. There were steep tariffs, strict quotas and lots of barriers. However, the world is now gradually moving towards economic and financial integration. Tariffs are being reduced and the volume of world trade has increased more rapidly than world production. There is also the beginning of an international labour market particularly for managerial, professional, technical and highly skilled labour.

In the 1980s the trend towards globalisation has got a new impetus. This has happened because of the growth of offshore financial markets, the increase in mergers and acquisitions and the growth of MNCs. The rapid technological changes and trends towards deregulation have resulted in the internationalisation of production. Because of global competition, many companies, especially the MNCs, have to use new technologies to adapt product characteristics for regional and local markets. All this has resulted in the reduction of state control or has forced governments to view their policies from the global, rather than the national, angle. The internationalisation of the currency markets has further limited the role of central banks to control the money supply. The ability of large firms to locate their fixed investments anywhere in the world has further reduced the role of the state in regulating interest through taxation, minimum wage legislation, environmental control and other regulatory mechanisms. All these trends have weakened the controlling ability of the state, unless it learns how best to manage a truly global economy.

Regionalism

Even as the world is moving towards globalisation, there is a simultaneous trend towards regionalism. As a result, the dividing line between free trade and protectionism is becoming increasingly blurred.

Investment Climate and Technology Transfer

There is more and more domestic investment, particularly in some of the developing countries with a view to gain control over

sophisticated technologies. At the same time, international investments are attracted to low cost countries with a view to conquering
global markets. What is to be seen is whether the new technological revolution will benefit only the developed countries or
whether the developing countries can also gain by capturing a
major share of the global market. A look at the East Asian countries, especially Japan, shows that this is possible. The question
remains whether other developing and underdeveloped countries can do the same. Malaysia, Singapore, Thailand or more recently, Vietnam, show that they can. However, the conditions
have to be favourable for investment. In this connection, we
made a study of four countries—Thailand, Singapore, Malaysia
and India—to compare the factors that favour or hinder investment patterns. The main factors that can affect investment are:

1. The development philosophy of the country;
2. Policies for industrial investment;
3. HRD policies; and
4. Other issues like the clearance procedures, infrastructure
   and fiscal and monetary policies.

The comparative analysis of the investment climate is given in
Table 9.1. The table indicates that the investment climate in Singapore and Malaysia has been highly favourable on almost all counts.
Thailand is also moving towards a favourable climate. However,
in India, the climate was obstructive, but is gradually being made
facilitative.

Technology Transfer

In today's context, technology determines the growth and development of any nation. Some countries, because of their innovative practices and inventions, have been able to develop
technology at a much faster pace resulting in better living standards for their people. However, there are a vast number of less
developed countries, which, for various historical reasons, could
not keep pace with technological developments. Also, with

TABLE 9.1 **Investment Climate of Countries**

Factors Affecting Investment	Countries				
	Thailand	Singapore	Malaysia	India
1. *Developmental Philosophy*	Thrust on economic growth to bring about social change	Open economy for faster growth	Accelerated restructuring of society to correct social and economic imbalances	Simultaneous social and economic change
2. *Policies for Industrial Investment*				
(a) Key expected benefits to the nation	Economic growth and export earnings	High-technology, export earnings and economic growth	Export earnings and technology	Technological self-sufficiency, satisfaction of domestic demand and exports
(b) Government intervention	To facilitate	To facilitate and encourage	To facilitate	To regulate and monitor
(c) Extent of intervention	Low, initially, and minimal after licensing	Low	Low, initially, and medium subsequently to ensure implementation of protective legislation	High initially and continues
(d) Instrument for intervention	Operating licence	Incentives and approvals	Operating licence and incentives	Operating licence, permits and quotas
(e) Location policy	Relieve urban congestion and provide infrastructure	Provide infrastructure, and encourage investment outside Singapore	Provide infrastructure and encourage regional development within the country	Promotion of regional development within the country

(f) Environment	Recent awareness and incentives being introduced	High government regulation with statutory norms	Clearance required along with operating licence	Separate approval from environment and pollution control board

3. *Other Issues Affecting Investment*

(a) Direct negotiation	Minimal	Intense negotiation by government for high technology	Minimal	Intense
(b) Time taken for clearance	Months	Months	Weeks	One to two years with exceptions (weeks/months)
(c) Location	Industrial estates in non-urban areas	Industrial estates encouraged	Industrial estates encouraged	Backward regions encouraged
(d) Infrastructure	Government responsibility	Government responsibility	Government responsibility	Companies are on their own
(e) Joint ventures	Required in some cases and otherwise encouraged	Encouraged specially for units located outside Singapore	Required in some cases	Encouraged and required in some cases
(f) Employment quotas	Not an issue	Not an issue	Some reservations for Bhumi Putras (sons of the soil)	Reservations in public sector and government organisations for certain categories
(g) Sophistication of technology	Encouraged through incentives	High-technology encouraged through special incentives	Encouraged through incentives	Encouraged

continued

Table 9.1 continued

Factors Affecting Investment	Countries				
	Thailand	Singapore	Malaysia	India	
4. Human Resource Development					
(a) Skill development and upgradation	Company's major responsibility	Huge government incentive and subsidy for skill upgradation	Partial government incentive for skill upgradation	Company's sole responsibility	
(b) Labour protection measures	Trade unions not allowed	Trade unions exist but concentrate on non-bargainable activities	Good protective legislation, control on direct action, union role minimal	Politically–affiliated and fragmented trade union movement, accent on collective bargaining or legal machinery	
5. Fiscal and Monetary Policies					
(a) Currency convertibility	Full convertibility with some restrictions on repatriation	Full convertibility and free exchange regulations	Free exchange regulations with some restrictions on repatriation	Partially convertible currency and restrictions on repatriation	
(b) Interest rates (1995)	High (10.7%)	Very low (3.4%)	Low (3.9%)	Very high (12.9%)	

changes in income patterns, and communications, it becomes a futile exercise for each country to develop its own technology from scratch. Some countries can develop their expertise and technology in certain areas, while others have different kinds of skills and resources to offer. Therefore, technology should be shared so as to achieve better living standards in all countries.

Any technology transfer is beneficial both to the country that transfers and the country that receives. While the developed countries have adequate R&D funds, technological know-how and necessary financial resources, they may not have the requisite facilities and markets. The developing countries, on the other hand, have bigger markets thanks to larger population and increasing purchasing power, but resources for investment and R&D are scarce. The transfer of technology, for value-added processes, from the developed to the developing countries, benefits both. Only 4 per cent of the world's R&D activity is conducted in the developing or less developed countries which account for 70 per cent of the world's population. On the other hand, 94 per cent R&D is conducted in the developed countries and the advanced technologies are being transferred only on a commercial basis. The issue of adopting indigenous technology poses several problems unlike the technology from developed countries. Indigenous technology may not have been proven yet or have plants in operation. In the case of transfer from laboratories to plants, it faces the additional problems of commercialisation and long gestation periods. Therefore, import of highly sophisticated technologies is less risky for industry. Indigenous technology development and self-reliance can also result in valuable time being lost and widening the technological gap between the developed and the developing countries. Another issue in transfer of technology is the constraints such as:

1. Non-availability of foreign exchange;
2. High cost of transfer; and
3. Problems of adapting to local conditions—the level of local skills available, socio-economic infrastructure and quality of locally-available raw materials.

These constraints can be minimised by identifying the appropriate technology and harmonising the needs of the transferees and the recipients. When the value-added processes are transferred, they may lack the integration usually found in modern organisations of the country of origin. Material and vendor items are costlier in developing countries because of inefficiency of the domestic transportation system, longer lead-time, higher inventory levels, etc.

Human Resource Development

The new industrialising economies are largely dependent on large-scale transfer of technology from the developed countries. As is evident from the examples of Singapore and Malaysia, the availability of a market or cheap labour may not always be the major incentive for foreign investors. The other factors attracting foreign investment and technology transfer can be the availability of proper infrastructure, investor-friendly policies and the capacity of the country to absorb foreign investment. Complaints by foreign investors about the lack of technology and skill transfer in recipient countries gradually declined as the countries gained experience with foreign investments and as their capacity to absorb foreign technology increased. The experience of some of the South East Asian countries is that investors will be motivated to transfer higher level of technologies depending upon the host country's capability to export. Singapore and Malaysia show that the host country can actively improve its capacity to absorb sophisticated technology by investing in education and training and by supporting the development of scientific and industrial engineering skills.

The method of technology transfer will be influenced greatly by the level of formal education and training in the recipient countries. There is a tendency among the developing countries to concentrate on professions like teaching, law and social sciences, while the requirement may be for agronomic, maintenance, technical, marketing and production skills. The transferors of technology therefore have an obligation to guide the recipient countries to revise their education and training policies in a way that will facilitate the successful acquisition of organisational and technical skills.

In order to absorb technology, HRD, especially the skill upgradation aspects, can be done in several ways. The experience of various countries suggests that they have been able to upgrade their skills by successfully adopting distinct approaches. The strategy adopted by the Middle East countries, which have the capacity to pay, is to buy the best technology and get foreign workers to operate this. Singapore, on the other hand, is encouraging foreign partnerships to help build up operating, repair and management skills geared to domestic and regional production. This strategy is mainly to develop skill-intensive activities in the country. The South Korean strategy has been to build up local, operating maintenance and management skills through the formation of foreign subsidiaries and joint ventures. Brazil depended upon the development of local skills with foreign direct investment partnerships, while in Mexico engineering and development skills were built up through joint ventures.

While technology transfer does help in skill upgradation and appropriate development of human resources, it can also create certain problems of personal interaction which need to be attended to in order to minimise adverse impact. Any sudden transfer of sophisticated technology can result in alienation among workers due to organisational or fiscal changes. Prolonged dehumanisation of work due to technology can also lead to a breakdown of functional patterns and give rise to discipline-related problems. This may necessitate an appropriate HRD approach at the micro level with an in-built system of career development, job enrichment, employee participation, to improve the quality of worklife.

There can also be resistance from the executives. Computerisation can minimise the importance of middle management and these cadres resist technological change. It is often observed that an individual's capability to learn new technology can decline after a certain age, even as demands to learn new techniques increases. High technology can also lead to problems of wage disparity by creating high-wage islands, both within and between companies.

To reduce all these problems, better HRD approaches, both at the macro and the micro levels, are needed. This will call for heavy investment in intensive training facilities for the middle management and enhancing the operators' skills through training and retraining facilities. A more effective interface between R&D and other related functions in an organisation also needs to be developed. There will be a need to provide training to customers, dealers, suppliers, etc. The organisation will have to create new HRD systems such as specialised cadres to encourage a technology-oriented culture to replace the traditional power and authority-oriented culture.

Any technology transfer can have both a positive and a negative impact on recipient countries. On the positive side, countries are compelled to take a re-look at their policies to give meaningful direction to industrial investment especially in sophisticated technologies. This also results in the opening up of new markets, availability of quality goods at cheaper prices, and pave the way for innovation of new products and better customer service due to increased competition. The other indirect benefit of technology transfer is upgradation of education and training institutions to cater to the required skills. Therefore, HRD also gets an impetus. So the economy gets a boost and there is a corresponding overall increase in employment and living standards of the people.

At the same time, the recipient country has to take into account certain negative factors that can adversely affect the economy in the short term and try to minimise their impact. The change in policies in order to bring in sophisticated technology can affect local enterprises, as imports may become cheaper. Domestic industry can also prefer to import technology instead of investing in indigenous R&D. This at times can also result in repeated purchase of similar technology without proper assimilation or absorption of the same.

While transferring technology, there is always a tendency to transfer some of the managerial practices and systems also, in

TABLE 9.2 **Impact of Technology Transfer**

Positive	Negative
1. Policies to give direction to industrial investment in high sophisticated technology	Disincentive to local entrepreneurs (imports are cheaper).
2. Increase in demand and opening up of new markets.	Reduced incentive for indigenous R&D.
3. Availability of good quality, cheaper products.	Redeployment problems due to new technology and new skill requirements—resulting in redundancies in some sectors and shortages in others.
4. Increased competition leading to product improvements and innovation as well as better service to consumers.	Emergence of new competition in domestic markets.
5. Long-term employment generation due to spurt in industrial investment and growth.	Problems due to restructuring of organisations because of technological changes.
6. Increase in demand for sophisticated skills—need for establishment of education and training institutions.	Human resource related issues: (a) obsolescence (b) wage disparity
7. Ultimate boost to the economy—more employment, better living standards, more export earnings.	(c) employee alienation and resistance to change

the belief that these concepts are universally applicable. But this does not always work and organisations are forced to make compromises. This also results in professed policies being quite different from actual practices.

While it may be easier to transfer and assimilate technological know-how, the transfer of managerial technology is more difficult because of the cultural differences. For successful technology transfer, it is crucial that proper adjustments are made in the managerial technology—manning norms, production yardsticks and appraisal systems—to suit the local environment and culture.

In the Asian environment, there may be certain limitations on human resource policies. For example, there is pressure to respect seniority or give preference to certain categories of people for employment like job reservations. In such a situation the employee appraisal system should be used mainly for employees' own development rather than promotions. The strong belief in seniority by tenure goes against the principle of merit-based seniority. In such a situation, the organisation has to ensure that the senior-most person also scores high on merit through appropriate training and developmental plans. Similarly, hire and fire policies will not be acceptable in a developing country. Systematic career planning right from the entry into the organisation, coupled with planned training and development, will ensure a satisfying growth for the people and the organisation.

Conclusion

Any large-scale investment in technology will necessitate structural readjustment to bring economic reforms in line with the industrial growth. Singapore, in the earlier stages of growth, had a major structural readjustment programme to open up the economy to foreign investors with the government developing a strong infrastructure base to facilitate clearance procedures and HRD through conscious policies of skill upgradation and training. Any structural readjustment programme, will have negative repercussions. But these can be minimised by adopting a proactive approach to the changes. While technology will make certain sections of the workforce redundant, the problem can be reduced by investing in skill upgradation training. Singapore and Malaysia have especially created skill development funds for this purpose. India has also created a National Renewal Fund. However, it has to be ensured that the fund is properly used to prepare people for the new jobs created by sophisticated technology. An exercise has to be conducted, both at the micro and macro level, to identify shortages in skills and then develop the necessary training programmes. Wherever appropriate, organisations will have to work out a redeployment policy as well as a voluntary retirement scheme (VRS) in collaboration with trade unions. With the entry of MNCs, the local industry will require additional incentives to sustain itself and grow. These incentives can be in technology consultancy as in Singapore or soft loans. The local industry can also get a boost with the MNCs providing technical know-how and training for the development of ancillary industries.

Ultimately, technology absorption and assimilation will be possible only if the recipient countries develop their own R&D base. This will call for defining an appropriate R&D policy by the government at the macro level including incentives for the research laboratories as well as industries. Developing countries may not have the appropriate resources for large investments in R&D. Therefore, it may be more appropriate to identify certain core areas and direct efforts towards them. There will also be need for an institutionalised mechanism of collaboration between educational institutions, including technical institutes, and the industry especially in areas of applied research.

10

Technology Transfer, Assimilation and Human Resource Development

A s was mentioned in the previous chapter, the pace of technological change is the key to the growth of any nation. Due to the varied patterns in income, communication and technological development in different countries, the sharing of technology has become imperative. With increasing globalisation, competitiveness has increased and many organisations lack the resources to develop technology on their own.

Alliances play a major role in bridging these technological gaps, increasing the interconnected product range, tapping new markets and meeting competition, servicing the customers better and above all saving time in developing new products and process technologies.

The need for alliances among organisations will help bridge the gaps in areas like R&D, manufacturing and marketing. The type of alliances entered into will reflect the objectives that are to be achieved.

Types of Alliances

R&D Alliances   Licensing agreements, cross licensing, technology exchange, visitation and research participation, personnel exchange, investment in joint development and technology acquisition.

Manufacturing Alliances   Original equipment manufacture, seconds sourcing, fabrication agreements, and assembly and testing agreements.

Marketing and Service Alliances   Procurement agreements, selling agents, servicing agents.

General Purpose Tie-ups   Standards coordination and joint ventures.

Technology Transfer and Assimilation

Technology transfer is the utilisation of an existing technique in an instance where it has not previously been used.

The absorption and assimilation of technology by the recipient organisation or country is the true yardstick of the actual transfer of technology. Otherwise it will be a mere transplant of technology for manufacturing/production purposes.

Therefore, it is important that the recipient organisation develops the capacity to utilise the technology on its own. Technology assimilation should be the major focus of recipient countries in order to derive maximum benefits from a technology alliance. True alliances should result in equal gains to both parties.

Process of Assimilation

Some important components of technology play a crucial role in the proper assimilation of technology. These are object-embodied technology such as facilities for testing, production and manufacturing, and design equipment; person-embodied technology with skills for operating, upgrading and unpacking technology;

document-embodied technology for providing the database to support design, testing, analysing and monitoring; institution-embodied technology to integrate the other three components, the organisation and government policies.

The Technology Atlas prepared by the United Nations Economic Social Commission for Asia and the Pacific (UNESCAP) has referred to these as technoware, humanware, infoware and orgaware. The major steps in technology assimilation comprise the identification of needs and sources of finance for investment, market demand and supply, technology forecasting, the availability of technology, the commercialisation, adaptation and upgradation of production.

The human component plays an important role in the assimilation process with infoware providing the basic support to assess the technology and make the appropriate choices.

The success of the technological alliance depends, to a great extent, upon the capability of the recipient organisation to receive technology. At times, the stronger partner may not be keen to increase the capability of the other partner, fearing the loss of its competitive advantage. They may offer training only in operations but not in the process; with the result that the junior partner is dependent on them for rectification of even minor defects. This blocks the process of assimilation and may, in some cases, eventually result in the break-up of the alliance.

The recipient organisation does not adequately prepare those who are identified for training with inter-organisational roles. Without a proper understanding of what the organisation is trying to achieve, the learning period is not fully utilised to gain maximum knowledge. Assimilation and absorption depend a great deal on learning being recorded systematically. However, often the documentation system is poor and since no records are maintained, cross-checking and verification become difficult.

Characteristics of Alliances in Indian Organisations

With the opening up of the Indian economy, alliances between Indian companies and MNCs can offer mutual benefits. Some of the advantages which Indian companies can offer are:

(a) Large domestic market
(b) Wide distribution network
(c) Reasonable manufacturing base/excess available capacity
(d) Relatively cheap labour
(e) Outsourcing of components at lower cost.

On the other hand, Indian organisations can gain the following:

(a) Continuous access to the latest technology
(b) Capital for investment
(c) Increased profitability
(d) Avenues for specialised training
(e) Prospect of joint ventures in third countries
(f) Marketing and services outside India

The focus of Indian organisations has been on short-term gains rather than long-term organisational learning, hampering the process of technology assimilation and upgradation on a sustained basis. This weakness of Indian organisations in assimilating and upgrading its technology has been to the advantage of their foreign partners, who are supplying updated technology on a continuous basis at increasingly higher prices.

Factors which Help/Hinder the Assimilation of Technology

1. *Investment in Human Resources* Improving the skills of employees to handle the increasing technological changes and developing sufficient design engineering capability to upgrade the existing technology is a critical factor in helping the assimilation process. Indian organisations should plan for the development of human resources along these lines in order to prepare for the challenge of competition.

2. *Increasing Trainability of Human Resources* The Technology Atlas defines the various stages of sophistication of increasing human abilities starting from operating, setting up, repairing, reproducing, adapting, improving and innovative abilities. All

these call for strengthening not only people's skill levels but also increases the capacity for training when they are performing the work in an organisation. With fast-paced changes in technology, the trainability component becomes more important than training people for a particular skill, the requirement of which may only be temporary.

The traits required for trainability include reasoning skills (development of cognitive ability); development of a scientific attitude; mastery of the appropriate language; development of communication skills; development of interpersonal skills; and self-discipline and responsibility.

3. *R&D Capability in India*   The involvement of R&D in the process of technology transfer, upgradation and innovation has been limited. Though most organisations do have an R&D department, it is set up mainly to avail various tax benefits. In some technologically advanced countries R&D plays an active role in receiving, unpackaging, and transferring technology to operations. However, in India, with a few exceptions, R&D has restricted its role to academic pursuits rather than applied research for commercial purposes. A more active involvement of R&D in operation-related activities can ultimately increase the bargaining power of Indian organisations.

4. *Long-term Planning for Technology Development*   If organisations want to survive in the long term, it is important for them to clearly define their short- and long-term technology development policies and work out their strategies accordingly. This will help in focusing the assimilation efforts on technology for the long-term growth of the organisation.

5. *Bargaining Capability*   In most technology alliances, the partners are not necessarily equal. Indian organisations can offer the market potential in order to bargain for access to the latest technology. The restrictive clauses with regard to upgrading and improving technology can be minimised through better negotiations.

6. *Competitiveness of the Organisations*   In order to keep abreast of the competitors and retain market share, constant upgradation and improvement of the products are imperative. This determines the pace of assimilation of technology and is also largely governed by the nature of the technology itself. For example, the pace of technological change in the electronics industry has been revolutionary as compared to some other industries.

7. *Documentation*   Poor documentation at times hinders the process of assimilation. There is no proper system of recording information about the various technological changes or modifications made in the process from time to time. While negotiating for alliances, it is often found that Indian organisations are unable to provide suitably updated documents about their existing technology capabilities.

8. *Functional Coordination*   For total assimilation of technology, proper functional coordination among operations, R&D, marketing and HRD is essential. The coordination between human resources and other functions is especially important with regard to the development of appropriate manning norms and identification of training needs for handling and absorbing the technology. Similarly, R&D, marketing and operations need to work very closely to understand the whole process and ensure constant upgradation.

The experience of other countries, especially South Korea, indicates that the understanding of the processes is much better when R&D professionals are fully involved in the entire transfer operation. In fact, in some South Korean organisations, the technology is initially transferred to the R&D department, which in turn transfers it to operations. The advantage of involving R&D from the outset is that it understands the process aspects and can consider upgrading the technology on its own wherever required.

9. *Infrastructure*   Suitable government interventions in terms of providing infrastructure services like transport, communication facilities, the legal framework, financial services, material testing

laboratories, and setting appropriate standards, are indirect factors affecting the process of technology assimilation. There is a definite need for industry–government collaboration to improve and develop these facilities.

Apart from training personnel for the operation of machines, technology transfer should include preparing personnel to operate and maintain some of the essential infrastructure facilities.

10. *Human Resource Readjustment* The government's labour policies can play a significant role in encouraging foreign investment, transfer of technology and technology assimilation. It is essential to put in place micro and macro level policies regarding redundancies, skill changes, redeployment, and related issues. While, at the macro level, the government has to ensure a conducive legal framework to protect the interests of all parties, at the micro level, each organisation has to work out its own readjustment policies.

In India today, there is little flexibility to redeploy persons due to technological changes because of resistance from trade unions. One of the ways of reducing this problem is the adoption of a participatory approach and working out a rehabilitation plan for each employee affected by technological change. Germany has a co-determination law which stipulates that the employees have to be informed in advance about any major technological changes being envisaged and the management has to work out a rehabilitation plan jointly with the employees' representatives. It is believed that this process has reduced the resistance to technological change in Germany as compared to some other countries like the United Kingdom or India.

11. *Lack of a Technology Assimilation Policy* In many cases, companies have not defined long-term technology assimilation as one of their missions or objectives. The result is that the organisations concentrate purely on technology transplant and meeting production targets.

12. *Equity Participation* Indian partners in most alliances have found that they had to compromise on their share in the total

equity participation because of their poor technology assimilation. The stronger partner (usually a foreign company) begins to insist on increasing its stake as a precondition for bringing in the latest technology and then emerges as a majority shareholder.

Case of Process Industry Limited (PIL)

PIL is one of the large chemical process companies in India with a sales turnover of Rs 22.79 billion. In 1989, PIL was rated as one of the best performing chemical companies in the world and in 1995 it was placed among the top 10.

PIL's major products are petrochemicals (plastics, synthetic rubber, synthetic fibre, industrial chemicals), advanced engineering plastics, catalysts, absorbents, wire and cable compounds, corrosion consultancy and external training contracts. It has around 30 plants spread over three locations. Most of these plants were set up through technology transfer agreements with some of the largest technical firms in the world.

It has almost 30 technology transfer agreements mainly with American and European companies. In addition, PIL has joint venture agreements with French and American MNCs for advanced engineering plastics. It has also formed joint ventures with large Indian companies for a part facility. PIL is also in the process of setting up a joint venture in Saudi Arabia and has an agreement to train technical personnel from Iran.

In the initial stages, PIL, as a policy, bought the technology on lump sum payment without any equity participation with a view to developing the technology itself. In most cases, the technology was bought as a packaged deal and no reverse engineering was undertaken. The agreements, the periods of which ranged between six and 15 years, had restrictive clauses with regard to technology upgradation.

Before 1995, investment through equity participation by the foreign partner was discouraged except in very specialised sectors. The situation changed after 1995 and PIL also entered into alliances based on 50 per cent equity participation with appropriate transfer technology alliances with American and French MNCs. The development of technical capability within PIL and its past performance were able to attract foreign investment, which, in turn, helped PIL to obtain the latest technology from its partners.

Most of the earlier technology transfer arrangements were packaged agreements where the licensors would provide only the production facilities and training in plant operations. The setting up of various plants was contracted out to engineering consultants by PIL. The training of the personnel was confined to operational aspects and not the process know-how. Therefore, adaptation skills were missing. The documentation of various technology agreements was weak, and the accessibility of available data for upgradation and improvements was, consequently, limited.

Nature of the Latest Joint Venture

However, in the more recent alliance with an American company, PIL is attempting to bring in a totally new work culture and has tried to rectify some of the problems faced earlier. This was done on the premise that the latest technology in advanced engineering plastics will be available. The American company, for its part, gained access into the hitherto protected Indian market. PIL has been in this field, using different raw materials and technology. The new plant was set up with a separate identity and every facility being independent of the existing plants. The head of the unit is one of the directors of PIL and the head of the manufacturing division has been recruited because of his experience in working with similar technology. The head of manufacturing, the quality assurance manager and other key personnel were given extensive training at the foreign partner's plant. The training combined both plant operations as well as courses in general management, marketing, and HRD.

The operations and quality departments in the new unit have been encouraged to bring in process modifications and product improvements. This has resulted in major savings, enhanced productivity, energy conservation, and product acceptability.

The manning norms have been decided with emphasis on job flexibility. There is a positive blending of the cultures of both the Indian and the American companies to keep the manning levels to the absolute minimum. The personnel have been selected giving importance to their technical competence and their innovative skills. The concept of multi-skilling has been introduced. The entire personnel of the plant are referred to as a manufacturing team and all operators/technicians handle both operations and maintenance jobs. This is in total contrast to PIL's work culture where operations and maintenance are treated as two distinct jobs.

This alliance has provided the Indian partner with the latest technology only while there are some restrictions on the market inputs. The market for the products of the new plant is restricted to the Middle East, South East Asia, India and its neighbouring countries. The present process also requires almost 80 per cent of the raw materials and components to be imported from the foreign partner.

The new venture has been set up with a view to introducing a more informal work culture. Creativity and innovation are encouraged. The work practices reflect a wide range of cultural forces—the attitudes of employees towards the new working style do not take place in isolation. PIL has a common uniform for all employees, as is the practice in the foreign partner's plants. It has also been promoting indigenous managerial capability in the plant to achieve performance standards.

The R&D centre is being set up at a different location to undertake application research and is headed by an expatriate. This centre plans to take up research relating to product applications, alternative raw material, etc.

This alliance of PIL has sought to overcome some of the technology-related problems by adopting better-defined strategies. The level of absorption of technology has been quite high though the actual extent of assimilation is yet to be calculated. There are no immediate plans for expansion as the market is yet to be explored and marketing strategies evolved.

Case Study of ABC Company

ABC Company is a diversified integrated corporation dealing with information technology (IT) consumer products, healthcare, systems engineering, lighting, financial services, etc. Here we will look at only the company's IT division. This division is the largest, with a total sales turnover of about Rs 3 billion (total sales turnover of the company is Rs 6 billion) and a profit of Rs 80 million.

The IT division has two wings—one dealing with computers and the other with systems. The IT division is considered to be one of the fastest growing software companies in India with exports to the tune of Rs 340 million. The company holds a major market share, offering the widest range of products in this line.

The company strategy has been to invest in R&D apart from entering into alliances with global leaders and technology providers like AT&T, Tandem, Sun Micro Systems and Intel. ABC ventured into the arena of IT in the early 1980s and gradually expanded its operations from services to technology and products. Initially, the company started with the import of hardware from Motorola and software from Intel and the assimilation and upgradation of these technologies. The company has progressed from merely adopting industry standards to implementation of sophisticated networking systems. The primary objective, however, remained increasing market share and keeping pace with the changes in technology. The focus has not been so much on technology development, innovation and sale of technical know-how.

ABC has positioned itself as a mediator between the various technology providers and technology packagers. They are not taking up basic research or applications research but are merely providing the intermediate support service for packaging and sale of these products. ABC customises or modifies the technology to suit the requirements of customers or end users and also provides the necessary support services. For example, it imports around 50 per cent of the hardware components and manufactures the end products by integrating the system with suitable user packages.

ABC has entered into different types of arrangements to suit business needs, like marketing alliances, technical know-how agreements, and providing qualified design engineers. The marketing alliances provide benefits like the distribution network and economies of scale. The exchange of qualified personnel is in terms of the training and sharing the experience of the latest technological developments in the organisation providing the technology. This kind of arrangement begins on a project-tied basis in order to establish an initial business relationship. It eventually resulted in the development of mutual trust and further collaboration. For example, in one such arrangement, the company was able to negotiate for the import of tools and basic technology for substantive value addition in its local unit. There has been a considerable build up of the knowledge and skill base as a result of this exchange. The engineers trained in specific areas abroad return to the organisation and in turn train groups in the usage of the latest systems and packages.

Human Resource Development

The ABC Company employs around 1,700 employees, 80 per cent of whom are qualified technical personnel. The organisation claims that it gives utmost importance to HRD and constant skill upgradation. It has developed a well-integrated system of internal and external training through both the annual performance appraisal report as well as an assessment by an external agency. The organisation claims that because of this emphasis on HRD, the turnover of its employees is only 12 per cent as compared to the industry average of 18–20 per cent. The organisation believes in internal growth and career planning of its personnel. Even in the case of new projects in diversified areas, the first priority is given to appointing existing employees with appropriate training rather than through external recruitment.

The organisation believes that the technology can not only be purchased but it can also be brought and assimilated by personnel who are sent abroad for training. They, in turn, also bring in the expertise to develop the similar technology themselves. The organisation has a well-developed system of job rotation in line with employees' interest, aptitude and career planning. The personnel are also rotated on projects abroad to provide learning opportunities to all. It is usually the practice to identify persons with at least four-five years experience in the organisation to be sent for training on projects abroad.

Research and Development

At ABC, R&D is considered important in the process of technology assimilation. The total expenditure on R&D was around 2 per cent of the total sales turnover. The company's R&D investment ranks amongst the top 50 R&D investments in India. This investment is focused on the frontier areas of technology enabling the company to build up a creditable skill and knowledge base and helping it forge strategic alliances with large MNCs. The company's R&D has an inherent strength in the development of micro and mini computers and in incorporating the latest technology. The level of assimilation has been high as the persons involved are highly qualified. As a result of these efforts, the company was able to design and launch several new products, some especially designed for the international markets. The company gives equal importance to R&D in relation to other departments. The R&D department works in close collaboration with the marketing division and is also closely involved, from the outset, in negotiations with clients and partners in technology.

The IT industry faces intense competition and technological obsolescence due to the rapid and phenomenal changes in recent years. ABC has, therefore, so far only strived to keep pace with the changes. In the process, it has been importing technology for value addition and sale without much stress on technology innovation or absorption. Assimilation has been done only to the extent that it was essential for upgrading or modifying the technology to suit customer specifications.

Factors that Help or Hinder Technology Assimilation in PIL and ABC Company

Assessment of Technology For any assimilation of technology, the recipient organisation must be able to appropriately assess the technology which it intends importing. This calls for a proper assessment of technology gaps through an appropriate database and by developing an institutional mechanism for such an assessment. This also entails upgrading the skills of human resources to analyse and upgrade information. In the initial stages, PIL did not possess sufficient technical competence to assess the technology sought to be imported. Over the years, PIL gained sufficient experience in related fields to source, assess and bargain for the best available technology. The earlier agreements were very biased towards the licenser and too many restrictive clauses were incorporated which hampered the upgradation of technology.

ABC Company follows a systematic procedure for the continuous assessment and updating of the latest technological developments and their market potential. It has been investing in upgrading human skills through research and training in frontier areas of technological development. Because of this, the company is in a better position to assess the global competitiveness of technology and also approach the technology developers. Awareness of latest market developments and customer preferences is necessary to keep pace with the changing technologies.

Internal Technology Development and Marketing Strategies In PIL, the process of assimilation was not focused on product upgradation and proper marketing strategies. It operated in a protected market and thus overlooked the need for forecasting technology development and suitably upgrading its skills. Now, the opening up of the economy has put tremendous pressure on exploring new markets. ABC Company operates in a highly competitive environment that has necessitated the adoption of aggressive and innovative strategies to retain and expand its market. There is a constant upgrading of technology and product features to suit customer needs with a back-up of support services to enhance the product's marketability.

Negotiating for Technology Alliance   The choice, evaluation and negotiation mechanisms are very crucial for any technology alliance. The PIL team for negotiating for technology is chosen on the basis of its expertise. At times, there are pressures from the government or the top management of the company to send persons for reasons other than expertise. There are also restrictions on the number of persons who can be sent for negotiations. For instance, in recent negotiations with a U.S.-based licenser, the negotiating team faced major problems in obtaining clearances for visit to the U.S. The government was willing to allow only two representatives and insisted on the director being one of them. After a lot of persistence, a three-member team was allowed. During the course of the negotiations, the U.S. company tried incorporating the restrictive 'Super 302' clause in the agreement. The 'Super 302' clause is a list of limiting conditions relating to technology transfer ratified by the U.S. senate in order to make other countries comply with its policies. It was here that the presence of the technical person helped. He was successful in arguing against the validity of the anti-trust clause, pointing out that PIL could obtain the technological know-how through the other Asian licensee of the American firm. Earlier, PIL had scrupulously observed the restrictive clauses imposed by the licensee.

Understanding the process aspect of technology is important for any assimilation and upgradation. However, in PIL, the transfer of technology was initially confined to the operational level as was the training given to the employees. Since the R&D had a limited role, the company repeatedly went in for further technical collaboration for any upgradation paying professional charges.

ABC Company builds the team for negotiation of alliances with persons having the best expertise. Their position in the office hierarchy is not the only criterion for selection. The negotiations are initiated very gradually after building up a rapport with the other organisation. For example, the ABC Company first provided only design experts to an American company to help them in designing and programming. Over a period of two years, after establishing a certain level of confidence and a positive working relationship, ABC Company approached the organisation for an alliance to operate from India.

The constitution of the negotiation team and the processes are often constrained by rules and regulations in the public sector, while the private sector has the freedom to select the best possible team as a result of which they are able to take faster decisions and get better terms.

Issues of Assimilation and Incentives   Though PIL has been successful in developing and commercialising certain technologies, it has not been successful in marketing its know-how. PIL found that the Indian market is biased towards foreign tie-ups, even though indigenous technology is available. Also, the company has not been aggressive in selling its technology.

The products dealt with by ABC Company require a high level of assimilation and upgradation of technology. The clients import the products and processes with a view to marketing them after suitable value addition and customisation. This, in itself, has been an incentive for constant upgradation of technology. The access to technology has been through training in organisations abroad and continuous involvement of R&D in all areas of business activity.

Interdepartmental Coordination and Role of R&D   At PIL, even after the transfer of technology, there is little interaction or coordination between R&D and operations. There is reluctance to share information and documentation.

PIL has a technology department that acts as a coordinating agency between the R&D and operations department. The department's role includes monitoring the production process, identifying areas for improvement and involving R&D in bringing in necessary modifications. The role of R&D is, therefore, restricted to some trouble-shooting, attempts at indigenisation of certain raw materials, enhancing/optimising consumption levels, etc.

The technology department's role can be more intensive at the time of technology transfer and the R&D department can gradually play a greater role along with the operations in improving and upgrading technology through closer monitoring. The technology and R&D departments can be merged so that the latter does not operate in isolation and can also take up more applied research activities.

In ABC Company, on the other hand, R&D has a role to play in all the major activities, including negotiations. Marketing and R&D are treated at par and work in very close coordination. The R&D department is very actively involved in technology development and applications research to improve product lines and features.

Marketing of Technology Capability R&D has so far made a few significant contributions in terms of developing certain catalysts and process modifications. PIL is now able to offer certain advances and improvements in the technology and has also shown greater potential for assimilation. This has helped it forge alliances with larger firms due to technical back-up and R&D inputs being available within the organisation.

ABC Company has established a reputation of trustworthiness and quality in global R&D and marketing capabilities. The technology, products and systems developed by ABC Company have been accepted in the international and domestic markets, for example, the UNIX operating system.

Human Resource Related Issues Another factor hindering the proper assimilation process is the manning pattern. In one of the studies conducted at PIL, it was found that around 30 per cent of employees, both at the managerial and the workmen levels, were surplus and a number of them had overlapping responsibilities. Proper caution is not exercised in matching the persons with the skills required at the project implementation stage. Further, identification of personnel and transfer decisions are delayed resulting in limited time being available for adequate preparation for the new job. The selection of persons for training, especially for programmes abroad, is based on seniority rather than skills needed by people to handle their jobs. In one instance, a senior manager in the personnel department was sent abroad for training on advanced welding technology simply because he was the senior-most person and it was his turn to undergo technical training. After his return, he was posted again in the personnel department and he retired from service within a year of his return. The entire training effort was therefore a waste. There were many similar cases within the organisation. This indicates lack of career planning, training and placement policies in the organisation.

While selecting people for handling new projects in PIL, previous training and experience in a particular line are not always insisted upon. This is partly due to the organisational culture of giving more persons the opportunity to handle new projects and undergo training. This results in the organisation not utilising the best available skills and expertise.

The trade unions and officers' associations play a major role in slowing down the proper assimilation and upgradation of technology by resisting change. In PIL, trade unions do not allow any redundancies to be declared due to technology change and minor process modifications. This hampers upgradation and technology change and indicates the lack of an appropriate redeployment policy.

ABC Company believes in proper training and development of personnel. The major problem remains the high turnover. Though this is lower than the industry average, it does present certain constraints. Career planning and growth paths are reviewed periodically to overcome the problems in succession planning. There is a systematic process of training needs identification to help the individual and the organisation in skill upgradation. The selection process for initial recruitment tries to maintain a balance between experience and newly acquired skills.

With the opening up of the economy and entry of MNCs into the market, the shortage of skills has led to very high salary and compensation packages in order to attract the best talent. ABC Company also had to increase its incentives, considerably adding to overall manpower costs.

Manufacturing Activities   Liberalisation and consequent changes in custom and import duties have drastically affected manufacturing operations in the IT industry. ABC Company has substantially reduced its own basic manufacturing activity as it has become simpler and cheaper to import the bulk of components and take advantage of the economies of scale afforded by larger manufacturers. This has affected technology assimilation to an extent.

Conclusion/Suggestions

Technology Improvement and Image Building   In several Indian organisations, the incentive for technology alliances/transfer is to get a foreign brand name that has a better saleability. This is always to the disadvantage of the Indian partner, especially when it is technologically inferior and the major incentive offered is the vast marketing potential. To overcome this problem, the organisation must, over time, develop long-term and short-term technology assimilation policies that will eventually help in building its image.

Building and Marketing of Indian Organisational Image   Some organisations do have the capability and competence to develop and innovate technology as was found in some areas in PIL. However, the organisation could not leverage this to its advantage. The organisation must make a conscious effort to build its image with regard to its present and potential technology capability. ABC Company has consciously established an image of quality and service, and concentrates on maintaining this.

Incentives for Technicians   In Indian organisations, the prospects for employees' growth are always higher in administrative jobs. Therefore, even capable technicians normally aspire for administrative work. In contrast, in South Korea, the technician can rise up to the master craftsman level by clearing certain examinations and meeting specific criteria. According to South Korean law, a master craftsman has to be paid a salary equivalent to that of a professor. This has enabled the specialised skills to be retained and improved within the organisation/country. It has also con- tributed to the reversal of brain drain.

Increasing R&D Involvement The involvement of R&D in tech- nology transfer and assimilation in India is weak. Even the R&D budgets are inadequate. In ABC Company too, R&D is given importance more to keep pace with the latest developments than for innovation and change.

Documentation Systematic documentation of the entire process of negotiation, transfer and technical details, including any up- gradation and modifications made, is essential. A proper docu- mentation of all relevant information enables simpler and quicker information sharing and review of the level of technological development. It also ensures continuity if employees leave.

Closer Collaboration between Government, R&D and Industry
As the financial resources for setting up R&D centres are limited, there should be closer collaboration between the government, R&D laboratories like the Council of Scientific and Industrial Research and the industry, especially to take up joint applied research projects. Some universities or technical institutions like the IITs can also collaborate with R&D laboratories by constituting research teams for specific projects.

Increasing the Trainability of Workforce More investments need to be made in skill upgradation and increasing the trainability of employees, especially in sectors like electronics where technology is changing rapidly. Some companies like ABC are investing in training mainly to meet their immediate needs and there is little investment for future skill development.

R&D Involvement The R&D personnel should be involved in any technology transfer from the beginning and they should be given the major responsibility of assimilation and upgradation.

Negotiation Capabilities   Many companies do not negotiate the technology transfer for the purpose of assimilation. Therefore, it is just a 'transfer' of packaged technology. Given the vast availability of qualified human resources in India, it is possible to gradually develop one's own capability for a more equitable alliance.

Blending for Technology and Adopting Indigenous Norms   At present, there is a wholesale transfer of technology including the manning norms and production yardsticks. However, these norms become inoperable due to deficiencies in the skill levels of employees and other operating conditions. There is a need for an appropriate blending of technology and, at the same time, the development of different norms and production yardsticks. For example, the manning norms and productivity yardsticks can be based on investment per man or production per unit of capital employed rather than man-hours.

A related issue is the employment and development of skilled professionals. Organisations must not only consider people's operating capabilities, but also their cognitive abilities to assimilate technology.

Role of Government Policies   In the past, government regulations restricted not only the transfer but also the assimilation of technology. With liberalisation, these regulations are being relaxed. Government policies should facilitate instead of regulating, as is the case in Malaysia and Thailand. These governments have taken the responsibility of providing infrastructural facilities, training the workforce, bringing in a more conducive legal framework for regulating employer–employee relations, and at the same time protecting employees' interests. A similar approach in India can help the assimilation process.

Cultural Factors in Transfer of Technology   While evolving human resource policies, given the limitations of recruitment and promotion, more emphasis has to be given to training. Similarly, the annual appraisal system can be used as a tool for development instead of only reward and punishment.

Incentives for Innovation   Companies must encourage and offer incentives for assimilation and innovation. In PIL's latest alliance, employees are being consciously rewarded with almost immediate effect, resulting in significant contributions from the operating staff in process modifications, better and simpler control systems, etc.

References

1. **Lorange, Peter,** 'Strategic Alliances: Formation, Implementation and Evolution', *Interim Reports for the Business Community (6),* International Labour Office, Geneva, 1992.
2. **Gruber** (1969) in **Stewart, J.R., Charles, T. and Yasumika, Nihei,** *Technology Transfer and Human Factors,* Free Press, New York, 1987.
3. **Brown, Halina, Derr, Patrick, Renn, Ortwin,** and **White, Allen,** *Corporate Environmentalism in a Global Economy—Societal Values in International Technology Transfer,* London, Quorum Books, 1993.
4. Committee on Japan, Technology Transfer, Competition and Public Policy, *US–Japan Strategic Alliances in the Semiconductor Industry,* National Research Council, Washington, D.C., 1992.
5. Asia and Pacific Centre for Transfer of Technology of UNESCAP, 'Technology Atlas—An Interim Report', *Asia-Pacific Technological Monitor,* March 1987.
6. **Virmani, B.R.** and **Guptan, Sunil Unny,** *Indian Management,* Vision Books, New Delhi, 1991.
7. **Virmani, B.R.** and **Rao, Kala,** *Economic Restructuring, Technology Transfer and Human Resource Development,* Second Edition, Response Books, Sage Publications, New Delhi, 1999.

11

Redefining Industrial Relations

The various members of the industrial relations system—the employers and managers, workers and their representatives, government departments—have institutionalised certain rules and regulations that govern the relationship between the employers and the employees.

But these rules were originally framed solely by the employers and were seen as being exploitative of the workers. The government was, therefore, compelled to step in on behalf of the workers. Simultaneously, the workers started moving towards unity and this led to the emergence of trade unions and the system of collective bargaining.

Collective bargaining focused on maintaining a balance of power between the parties concerned. It was characterised by a mistrust on both sides, withholding of information and the use of pressure tactics. However, this adversarial relationship, and consequently the nature of collective bargaining, is becoming irrelevant in the changed economic scenario. There have been far-reaching changes in the pattern of investment in industry, emergence of special interest groups like consumers and the public, a redefinition of the whole master–servant relationship between employers and employees. Therefore, the whole industrial relations system needs to be reviewed. But before doing that, it is important to analyse the historical background and evaluation of management concepts as well as the industrial relations system that evolved in other countries and was followed in India.

Historical Evolution of the IR Systems and Collective Bargaining

During the early stages of industrialisation, organisations were small and were proprietary ownerships. The proprietor had full control over the business and employed a minimum number of persons. However, new inventions led to mass scale production and the proprietor employed larger number of workers at various levels. That, in turn, created the need for supervisors and middle level managers to help him with the production process and keep a control over the organisation. Thus, certain systems of control, delegation and information emerged. Gradually a theory of management evolved, based on planning, organising, directing, controlling, coordination, etc. However, the basic premise was still that the proprietor is the master and the rest his servants. Labour was treated as a factor of production that could be manipulated in the same way as the two other major factors—land and capital. This concept also gave certain rights and prerogatives to the owners. This led to the employees coming together as a collective bargaining force. Faced with this collective pressure, the proprietor or his representatives agreed to negotiate terms and conditions of work. Collective bargaining became the governing principle of the industrial relations system and continues even today. The collective bargaining system, which evolved in Europe and was copied elsewhere has three distinct features:

1. It is based on a balance of power and the party which has the upper hand at any point of time always wins;
2. A certain amount of mistrust and withholding of information to win bargaining points; and

3. Threats of strike, lockouts and other forms of direct action which keep the dialogue going.

The whole system is based on an adversarial relationship with a view to getting the maximum out of the other party. It is common to withhold certain financial information from the other side. Often the employers deliberately misrepresent the financial and trading position of the company. At the same time, there is always pressure on the union leaders to prove that they are doing something for the employees they represent. The union is a highly political agency.

Present Structures of IR Systems

Each organisation develops its own special structures to deal with unions and collective bargaining. These structures are overlapping and inter-related and are perceived as 'good' or 'bad' from different angles. The major ones are:

The Structure of Balance of Power   Here, both parties exert all the pressure they can to get the maximum advantage by warning about the economic implications of a possible breakdown in talks. Each side accepts the other as a sovereign spokesman for its side.

The Structure of Containment   In this, the union aggressively presses to extend its scope of action and the management strives with equal determination to contain it within bounds. Bargaining issues are strictly confined to the limits set by law. The management gives in as gradually as possible. The scope of negotiations is rigidly defined and confined to traditional subjects like wages, hours of work, and conditions of employment.

The Structure of Conflict   This arises with the management refusing to deal with the union, though these days it has become a secondary pattern. However, employers are still determined to bar unions by all means at their disposal. They may deal with unions under pressure but never really accept them.

The above structures are considered to be on the left side of the balance of power. Power is used to work out an uneasy coexistence and parties are always on the verge of a showdown. Structures on the right side of the balance of power are expected to promote positive relationships. These are:

The Structure of Accommodation Managements and unions find their co-operative approaches to be the traditional agenda of collective bargaining like wages, hours of work and conditions of employment.

The Structure of Co-operation This is characterised by the parties extending the areas of mutual concern beyond familiar matters of wages and hours of work. They recognise productive efficiency, the solvency of business and the advance of technology as part of their common interest. The management also recognises its stake in a stable and effective union. The differences are healthy and relate to the interests of the organisation. However, such structures are difficult to sustain in an atmosphere of collective bargaining based on an adversarial approach.

The Structure of Deal Bargaining This requires a high degree of co-operation and understanding between the management and the union leaders. It is limited to top leadership and could be a source of strength as well as weakness. It involves secret diplomacy and is not recorded anywhere. Such deal negotiations are fairly prevalent.

Until now, we discussed the structures which are considered legitimate and within the legal framework. There are structures that are characterised by the exploitation of power in an illegitimate, illegal and immoral manner. Such structures are:

The Structure of Collusion Though collusion is a form of co-operation and deal bargaining, it is usually against the legitimate interests of the employers, the workers and the public. The management arrives at some underhand deal with the union. However, these days watchful competitors, rival unions and workers make such collusion difficult. But they still happen, especially in small undertakings.

The Racketeering Structure   In this, there is collusion between trade union leaders, criminal elements and corrupt politicians to impose a certain kind of industrial relations upon the industry. The coal sector in certain parts of the country has seen such structures.

The Structure of Ideology   The union clings to its own political ideology. Such structures may not accept the system of collective bargaining nor even Indian democracy. However, with the collapse of communism, the ideological structures are no longer advocated very strongly.

Compromise—The Backbone of Present Industrial Relations Systems   Whatever structure is adopted to settle the terms of co-operation, an adversarial relationship remains the backbone of the present industrial relations system.

Any method of imposing or dictating a decision invites immediate challenge, a fact that is well illustrated by the relationship between the employers and the workers throughout the growth of our industrial system. Where such a challenge is strong enough to demand negotiations, a relationship of competitive rivalry for domination is created. In such a climate, the usual method of reaching a decision is that of compromise. Authority is derived from the relative strength of the parties involved. But the results of such negotiations may be unsatisfactory for a number of reasons. First, a compromise seldom provides a solution to the real problem; it only appears to postpone the resolution of fundamental issues. Second, negotiation encourages rigid stances that inhibit frank discussion. Third, compromises made seldom satisfy any of the parties involved. People come away with the feeling that everything was decided beforehand and if the solution fails, the other party is blamed.

Frederick H. Harrison and John R. Cleman have stated that in many segments of mass production industries, collective bargaining is an orderly but continuous struggle for power between the management and the unions. In these conditions, collective bargaining is a somewhat negative process—a means of compromise and containment of conflict rather than as a vehicle for achieving common goals. It is a kind of an 'armed truce' relationship. Both sides spend time and energy bolstering their own positions and the resolution of differences depends on the relative power of the parties. In the Indian scenario, the emphasis has been on arriving at some sort of a deal bargaining with the union leaders rather than negotiating with the rank and file workers. There has been a tendency to have centralised negotiations at the headquarters at times even risking the displeasure of the local leadership.

The industrial relations scenario has not changed very much over the years. There have been attempts at reforming the plethora of legislation but these have failed mainly because both the trade unions and even the employers have adjusted themselves to the present systems and feel threatened by any changes in the structures. The involved parties seem to have developed a vested interest in maintaining the status quo. Efforts to make some modifications in the industrial relations scenario have been confined to some cosmetic changes in labour laws and not the transformation of the entire approach to industrial relations.

Trade Union Power Dynamics

There is an emerging trend where the trade union rank and file is asserting itself. A conflict between the established leadership and the emerging leadership is bound to arise. This, in the short-run, is expected to worsen the trade union power dynamics within organisations, lead to further multiplicity of trade unions and exacerbate inter-union rivalries, till such time as the trade union movement stabilises. Therefore, the next decade is not likely to present a peaceful industrial relations scenario. It is in this context that collective bargaining trends have to be viewed. Also so long as an adversarial and collective bargaining approach remains the mainstay of the industrial relations system, one cannot foresee a very healthy and peaceful industrial relations scenario in the future.

Collective Bargaining vs Participative Management

During the last few years, a feeling has emerged that the ultimate basis of organisations is co-operation and not conflict. Some countries tried alternative models that are more positive like co-determination in Germany. Also, with growing awareness about their rights, workers have begun to demand a say in managerial decisions which affect them. This was supported by social scientists who felt that such a system would help bring greater work satisfaction and commitment to work. Thus, there emerged an industrial relations system based on collective bargaining and principles of participation.

There is one view that the basic objective of an industrial relations system is to ensure that there is a harmonious relationship between the actors that comprise the system; there is no abuse of power as the interests of all the parties are duly protected. While collective bargaining is based on power dynamics and pressure tactics, participative management is based on trust, information sharing and mutual problem solving. Many trade unionists, academicians and managers both in India and abroad believe that industrial relations issues could be divided under the two heads and that both systems can coexist. However, there are others who believe that the watertight division of the issues will ultimately leave both the parties confused.

The ILO and many academicians and trade unionists strongly feel that collective bargaining is in itself a form of participative management. However, if this argument is accepted, then any talk of other participative structures like joint committees, works councils and joint management councils, becomes meaningless, because the strategies and tactics adopted by the parties concerned in both the institutions are usually different and have different outcomes (see Figure 11.1).

Keeping in mind the strategies and outcomes of collective bargaining and participative management, it can be argued that 'bargaining and negotiations' are the very antithesis of 'participation and consultation', and collective bargaining, in real terms, cannot be regarded as workers' true participation in the management or in the decision-making process.

FIGURE 11.1 **Nature of Relationship between Labour and Management and Its Impact**

Nature of Relationship	Strategies/Tactics	Outcome (Quality of Industrial Relations and Attitude of Parties)
1. Collective bargaining	1. Pressure tactics	1. Compromise agreement proportionate to the parties' strength
	2. Use of strengths	2. Lack of feeling of joint responsibility
	3. Withholding of information	3. Perpetuation of relationship based on suspicion and mistrust
2. Participative management	1. Mutual collaboration	1. Agreements integrating the interests of the parties involved and the needs of the situation
	2. Use of facts and figures	2. Feeling of joint responsibility
	3. Frank sharing of information	3. Perpetuation of the relationship based on mutual trust and confidence

Adversarial Approach—A Threat to a Positive Industrial Relations System and Participative Management—Some Case Studies

Considering the adversarial relationship of the two institutions, an in-depth study was undertaken of eight public and private sector organisations which claimed that they practised both collective bargaining and participative management. The purpose was to find out whether there are any conflicts between the two and how they affect each other. Of the eight, two were large steel manufacturing companies, one an aluminium manufacturing unit, one a public limited electrical company, and two were central government services departments.

Major Findings of Case Studies

In all eight organisations, both collective bargaining and participative management were practised. Though participative structures existed on paper, both the management and employee nominees did not perceive them to be real decision-making forums.

In several organisations, the trade union leaders perceived these forums to be a threat to their survival even though they themselves represented the employees on these committees. Hence, more often than not, they discouraged the workers from bringing issues to these joint committees for resolution. On the contrary, they often informally advised the workers to approach the union leaders who would then get matters sorted out quickly, at a personal level, with the management. The management also encouraged this. Therefore, by and large, the workers did not consider these participative bodies as forums where problems can be sorted out.

In most organisations, issues were clearly defined as falling under collective bargaining and participative management. Productivity increase and welfare issues were assumed to be part of the participative forums. Even in productivity-related issues, the primary focus was on the labour component and not on management-related matters. As a result, many participative bodies started with big fanfare but gradually interest waned, and after some time it became difficult to persuade members to even attend meetings of the various committees.

In two large organisations, any issue that had financial implications was to be decided at the bargaining table, and others in the participatory committees. However, it was found that every issue ultimately had some financial implications. For example, the issues of deteriorating standards of teaching in the primary school run by the company and the smelly toilets in the workers' colony were taken up for discussion. It was found that the quality of teaching was poor due to low salaries, and the toilets stank because of faulty construction. To remedy the situation in both cases would involve a financial burden, and therefore, the union and management agreed that these issues be taken to the bargaining table. Both these organisations claim to have a number of participative committees. However, over the years, these have degenerated into forums for discussion of neutral issues which involve third parties, like the removal of stray dogs by the municipality or improving cleanliness of roads by the corporation. Even if substantive issues were discussed, no decisions were allowed to be taken.

Union leaders at times found themselves playing contradictory roles. On the one hand they share information and participate in the decision-making process of the organisation; on the other, they use pressure tactics to extract the maximum out of the management at the bargaining table. The managements also find that their bargaining capacity gets eroded once the information is shared with workers' nominees at participatory forums. This discouraged managements from sharing any information in participatory committees. With such feelings of mistrust, it was found that these participative forums ultimately degenerated into mini negotiating bodies, complete with threats, counter threats, slogan shouting and strikes. This was more pronounced in some central government organisations. Where this went too far, the government even became reluctant to call regular meetings of such forums as was stipulated.

In several cases, the union leaders took up issues affecting a large number of workmen which fall in the realm of participative forums separately at the collective bargaining forum. It was on these issues that the leaders felt that they would get adequate support of the workers. This did happen in most cases, thereby increasing the bargaining power of the union leaders. In a number of such cases, the worker representatives went along with the union leaders, because they were themselves nominated by the union executive members. Also, they feared that not supporting the union leaders would make them unpopular with the mass of workers.

In the two government-run transport organisations, both the collective bargaining and participative bodies functioned simultaneously but there was no demarcation of issues. This often resulted in confusion. As a result, union leaders raised issues in one or the other forum depending on where they were strong at a particular moment. The management also did the same. The tactics adopted in participative bodies were the same as those used in the bargaining situation.

In a number of units, the local level union leadership favoured participation, while the senior-level leadership, which was drawn from outside and had political affiliations, was opposed to it. Some national level trade unionists went to the extent of saying that the formalisation of participation in the industrial relations system will sound the death-knell of collective bargaining and consequently trade unionism, and, therefore, they would never allow any other institution to come up. However, the rank and file workers and local leadership in almost all the organisations felt that the trade unions exist not for their own sake but for the workers. If the workers can have a say in the decisions that affect them, then the trade union would have to think of its role in a different context—in non-bargaining activities which would help enrich the workers' life. Therefore, the resistance of external leaders to participative structures can be attributed more to their vested interest than to concern for workers' welfare.

Collective Bargaining Leads to Third Party Intervention

An issue that has been worrying the trade unions is the relationship between the collective bargaining process and the participative management.

From the earlier discussion and findings, it is seen that collective bargaining and participative management have vastly different impacts. The former appears to have negative effect on the industrial relations systems, the economy, growth, and development, while the latter fosters a positive relationship between the involved parties. Collective bargaining may promote vested interests, while participative management promotes the interest of the working class as a whole. Since collective bargaining has negative implications, and a developing country like India cannot afford to stretch it too far, it leads to a situation (see Figure 11.2) in which collective bargaining based on power dynamics results in the involvement of the state to correct the power imbalance, the dependence of workers on outside leaders, politicisation of trade unions, inter-union rivalry, and third party intervention. So contrary to common belief that collective bargaining strengthens the rank and file trade union, it actually appears to weaken the trade union's bargaining power, and the shop-floor trade union leaders turn to politicians, the government and third parties to settle any differences. This state of affairs is hardly conducive for the development of a healthy relationship between the players in any industrial relations system.

In the final analysis, one cannot divide issues into two water-tight compartments—one, where there will be understanding and trust, and the other, where there will be mistrust and tussles. In the process of encouraging and strengthening both, we will end up weakening them, gradually allowing outside forces to take over to the detriment of the working class. The choices are, therefore, clear: If we want participation, then collective bargaining and the role of trade unions will have to undergo a meta-morphosis. On the other hand, if we want collective bargaining, we should stop talking of participative management; but this will be at the expense of the country's economic development.

Is Collective Bargaining Relevant Today?

With changes in the economic scenario and the pattern of ownership, the whole concept of owner and servant needs to be redefined in today's context. In public enterprises, everyone, including the top management, can be termed as servants. In private enterprises also, the investment by the promoters may be marginal and most of the funds may be borrowed. The so-called owners are in most cases managers, rather than owners, of the enterprise. Therefore, the old concept of an adversarial relationship and collective bargaining is becoming irrelevant.

In the 19th century when this concept of collective bargaining was evolving, the fear of the organisation being forced to shut down compelled the parties to arrive at a settlement. The adversarial approach was stretched only up to a point. However, in today's environment the fear of closure is not there to that extent. Even if a unit closes down, the employers do not stand to lose much as they have a marginal stake. Therefore, one can question the very relevance of collective bargaining as an industrial relations system in today's environment.

Alternative Approaches to the Theory of Management and Industrial Relations

Considering the changing pattern of industries, the classical definition of management based on the manager's prerogative to plan, organise, direct and control needs to be redefined due to the emergence of various interest groups including trade unions, consumer forums, and the general public. In the changed circumstances, the managers find it difficult to exercise these prerogatives. We need to develop a theory of management which defines 'how do we manage without any managerial rights or prerogatives' or 'how do we manage with the consent of people whom we are managing'. The western world is yet to evolve a satisfactory new definition of management in the changed context. Therefore, today's managers are finding themselves in an awkward position, where on the one hand they believe that they have managerial rights and prerogatives but in reality they are powerless to exercise any of those rights. Certain academicians and theorists are trying to develop alternatives to the outdated classical definition of management, based on participatory models, but nothing satisfactory has emerged as yet. Therefore, western management today is passing through a crisis period where the old model of management is dead and the new model is yet to be born. Some are taking refuge in the Japanese model which tries to blend the traditional value system with the current management concepts. For example, if seniority is to be respected then the senior-most person's competence must be honed through heavy investment in training and development. Similarly, selec-

FIGURE 11.2 **Clash/Conflict between Collective Bargaining and Participative Management and the Role of Third Party Intervention**

Stage I	Stage II	Stage III
Collective bargaining leads to a conflict–based relationship and mutual suspicion	Introduction of participative forums to improve the nature and quality of the relationship	Clash/conflict of participative forums with collective bargaining forums, trade unions

Stage IV

Trade union/management opposition at the time of introduction of participantive forums	Mutual suspicion/fear/continuation of bargaining orientation/role conflict	Inroads into scope of the participative forums and dilution of authority	Jurisdictional conflict of participative forums with collective bargaining	Opposition of trade unions if worker representatives on participative forums do not toe the line of trade union. Nomination of worker representatives on participative forums by trade union leaders	Inadequate sharing of information	Issues taken up at a personal level by trade unions and managements

Stage V	Stage VI
Pushing of participative forums to the background and perpetuation of conflict/mutual suspicion-based relationship between management and trade unions	Third party intervention to settle industrial relations problems

tions and placements have to be in line with the strengths of individuals. However, other countries, especially in the West, are unable to transplant such models partly due to cultural differences and partly because people find it difficult to give up the traditional approach which the government, trade unions, employers and academicians have been advocating for years.

In any model of industrial relations, the adversarial approach and collective bargaining must give way to participative structures or other institutions that check the adversarial approach. The U.S. tried to tamper with collective bargaining by developing Independent Neutral Arbitration Boards. Germany took refuge in an all comprehensive law on co-determination which is gradually replacing collective bargaining which itself is changing. The trade union leadership resists any structural changes as it feels it can thrive in the adversarial approach. Countries like Germany, Singapore and Malaysia reported an initial fall in trade union membership with the decline of the adversarial approach. However, they had to redefine their role and started concentrating on non-bargainable activities to enrich workers' life which led to a gradual increase in membership. Countries like Malaysia, Singapore and Thailand which have achieved almost full employment level without any workers' exploitation, do not believe in the traditional adversarial approach. However, the government played a crucial role in ensuring that the workers' interests are protected without the disruptions in the production activity that normally follows collective bargaining.

The international experiences worth emulating are the American, erstwhile Yugoslav and German systems, apart from some approaches adopted by Singapore and Malaysia. Some believe that the U.S. method of strengthening the collective bargaining system is ideal but unfortunately over 40 years of efforts in this direction have not left us with any hope. Further, our legal and other systems are moulded on the British pattern and the pitfalls in pursuing this line are obvious. The British system emphasises the collective bargaining process while allowing, at the same time, for some formal participative forum. The emphasis on collective bargaining has only led to a spate of crippling strikes. A developing economy cannot afford to follow this system any longer. And the system of workers' self-management in erstwhile Yugoslavia, though unique, is not possible in a mixed economy like ours. Germany, which had problems similar to ours in some respects, is experiencing comparatively better industrial relations and better productivity than other European countries. The other alternative is the Malaysian type of a highly protective system for labour to prevent exploitation along with legal restrictions to ensure there is no disruption of production. For example, strikes are not allowed for the first few years in a new enterprise.

In India, two alternative approaches can possibly be adopted. One is that the government follows the Malaysian model of enacting a highly protective legislation for employees and, at the same time, limits the scope of direct action. Alternatively, a partici- patory model can be developed in which issues are settled not through collective bargaining but mutual integration of interests with full sharing of information. The government may have to bring in a comprehensive scheme initially through legislation.

Need for Change in Company Laws

Another major issue having a bearing on the employer/man- ager's approach to participation is the definition of a company in the Companies Act which, in turn, is based on the 19th century British concept. This definition does not distinguish between a small and a large limited liability company. In fact, it does not dis- tinguish even between nationalised industries and other com- panies covered under the legislation. There may be need for some fundamental changes in the company law.

There are two basic problems to be tackled, which are relevant to the industrial relations system. The first is the concept under the company law that shareholders own the firm; and the second is that the general body meeting is the forum for decision making in companies. In reality, however, the general body meetings are very formal occasions and they are not forums for bargaining or participation. Most of the general bodies meet once a year and for a very short period. The shareholder with a large block of shares, is in an effective position, but not the one with a few shares. An employee at least attends office for over 300 days in a year, whereas the small shareholder probably never sees it.

The present shareholding structure of the Indian companies is diffused. This came to limelight during the controversy over the D.C.M. and Escort groups of companies a few years ago and in the ITC case recently where certain companies tried to take over these groups through aggressive buying of shares in the stock market. Most of the shares are held by public institutions and not the so-called owners or managers. In such a situation the stake in the company of the so-called 'shareholders' and of the top managers may be marginal. It is the employees and the general public who have the major stake and are likely to be most affected by any organisational decisions. In the present structure, there are four contestants for power in a company. The first is the shareholders. The second is the top management and some claim that the real power lies with them. However, company law does not recognise the management as a power centre but more or less as part of the company. One cannot say that managerial powers have a place in the framework of company law, as managers can be as vulnerable as workers.

The third power is the worker. The fourth power about which a lot has been heard lately but which does not have a strong spokesperson, is what can be called social or public interest. It is interpreted variously as 'the consumer', 'government policy' or 'the state'. Whatever the issue—whether it is consumer protection, a national wage policy, pollution—this fourth power needs to be integrated with company policy through legislation. The difficulty is how to translate consumer interest or social interest in the management in legal terms. The law already has a great deal of difficulty in separating the director as a person from the director as an agent of the shareholders. What needs to be considered is that the law must ensure that the directors behave as agents of shareholders.

Therefore, it is difficult to think in terms of institutionalising and defining management or even the worker. There are two differing views here. When the trade unions talk about workers, they are really talking about trade unionists, whereas most managements talk about their workers, whether or not they are trade unionists. There is also the problem of institutionalising the consumer or state interest. The German participative scheme, which has a supervisory board, was an attempt to institutionalise these interests with the concept of management, worker and community representative. We, in India, with the British attitude of laying emphasis on collective bargaining, will have much more difficulty in transforming such a system that is based on a conflict-oriented bargaining culture into a system of advisory forums where these interests can express their views. In spite of all these problems, any framework evolved has to take into account the financial interests of owners and shareholders and this has to be balanced with the interests of the workers, management, and the country.

The starting point from the management angle could be some compulsion on the management to share information with the workforce. Many companies may find this contrary to the duty of the company to its shareholders, who should get this information first. However, this old concept of shareholders' interest being supreme does not hold good in the new context.

Role of Trade Unions, Management, Government and Academicians

If the adversarial and collective bargaining approach has to be replaced by alternative models, then the role of the involved parties has to undergo a metamorphosis. An important question that arises is whether the trade unions will lose their control over labour. While the fears may be genuine, they may be less appealing if viewed in the overall perspective. The alternative approaches may offer less scope for the multiplicity of unions and labour militancy but the need for trade unions will still be felt. The trade unions can confine themselves to social matters rather than the economic matters. But the role will not be reduced to an enviable extent. It is believed that with workers' participation in management, the collective bargaining process will reform and become more responsible and productivity-based.

The trade unions, on their part, will gradually change their roles. They will have to give greater attention to non-bargaining activities to enrich the workers' lives. In addition, they will have to strengthen the capacity of the workers and their representatives in participative forums to play a more effective role rather than directly fighting over day-to-day matters. The trade unions can play a major role in workers' education, upgrading their skill levels and the capacity to participate more effectively in decision-making processes in the organisation.

The management's role will also undergo a transformation. With the involvement of the workers, some of the decisions taken by the middle management may shift to the participatory forums. Also with computerisation and other technological changes, some of the major decisions and information vital to decision-making will get limited to few middle and top level personnel eliminating the need for too many hierarchies. There will also be greater need to disseminate information to the participatory committees from which the management may derive the authority to take decisions. Therefore, it will be desirable to review organisational structures with a larger span of controls. Also, in the changed scenario, the management and unions together will have to increase the trainability of workforce by continuously upgrading their skills.

In the initial stage of transformation, the government may have to play a more active role. As the case studies show, both the union and the management would like to preserve the prerogatives and independence they enjoyed under the collective bargaining system. Therefore, the government may have to introduce and nurture the new institutions. Any voluntary effort may not entirely succeed as is evident from the examples of Germany, Singapore, Malaysia and the U.K. Even if there are stray examples of success, these have to be institutionalised as has been done in Germany, Malaysia and Thailand.

Academicians who have been reared in the tradition of classical definition of management and collective bargaining may have to do research in alternative models of management which are more relevant in the present context. The prerogative-based management will have to be substituted with a theory of management that is more participatory. Collective bargaining can no longer be a sacred cow and will have to be given up as a fundamental principle of the industrial relations system.

References

1. **Flanders, A.**, *Industrial Relations: What is Wrong with the System? An Essay on its Theory and Future*, Faber and Faber Ltd., London, 1962.
2. **Harrison, Frederick** and **Clemen, John R.**, 'Goals and Strategy in Collective Bargaining' in Healey, James J. (Ed.), *Creative Collective Bargaining— Meeting Today's Challenges of Labour Management Relations*, Prentice Hall Inc., New Jersey and Englewood, Cliffs, 1965.
3. **Virmani, B.R.**, *Participative Management vs Collective Bargaining*, Vision Books, New Delhi, 1988.
4. **Virmani, B.R.** and **Guptan, Sunil Unny**, *Indian Management*, Vision Books, New Delhi, 1991.
5. **Virmani, B.R.** and **Rao, Kala**, *Economic Restructuring, Technology Transfer and Human Resource Development*, Second Edition, Response Books, Sage Publications, New Delhi, 1999.

Managing Transformation: Indian Initiatives in Organisational Change through Networking— Case of the Oil Sector

The public sector oil and petroleum companies have been enjoying almost a complete monopoly in the country. However, over the last few years, the sector has been opened up and private firms (domestic as well as foreign) have been allowed entry into the oil sector, bringing in a competitive environment. The industry had been enjoying protection due to the Administered Price Mechanism (APM) which is gradually being dismantled. Thus oil firms are undergoing a major transition to meet competitive challenges. The competing oil and petrochemical firms are trying a unique experiment of networking and synergising their efforts in order to gain common advantage. This chapter looks at how the public sector oil companies have come together in certain areas to meet the competitive challenges and are trying to effectively manage change by involving their employees at all levels with the help of external resource persons.

Need for Networking for Organisational Changes

Considering the importance of the petroleum sector, there was a felt need for integrated action among oil companies to ensure oil security, consumers' interests and overall efficiency. A proposal was mooted in 1991 to set up a National Academy of Petroleum Management, on the lines of National Defence Academy, for senior executives in national oil companies and in governmental departments concerned with the petroleum sector. The idea was that the academy would provide a platform to augment information sharing, training, and seconding of expert manpower and crisis management capabilities to meet the challenges of the future. There were even some suggestions that the academy play a role in developing a petroleum sector culture with its own business needs and common standards of productivity, product quality and customer services.

To give shape to all these ideas, the heads of personnel of public sector oil companies suggested the constitution of a steering group to define the nature, scope and objectives of the proposed academy and recommend actions to operationalising them. A steering group was formed which, at its second meeting in February 1993, approached ASCI to help in conceptualising the main objectives, scope and immediate action plans. ASCI, along with the steering group, organised a specially designed inter-corporate workshop to elicit the views of the representatives of the companies with a view to develop conceptual perspectives for the proposed academy.

At that stage it was also felt that due to national and international developments, the idea behind setting up the National Academy of Petroleum Management may have to be reconsidered. Consequently, the canvas was widened to examine the logic of inter-corporate networking in the light of new opportunities and threats as well as examining the issues concerning operationalising the networking. The workshop thus aimed at enabling the representatives of the oil companies to:

1. Understand and assess the nature of the emerging global and national scenarios and the strategic role of the existing industry-level organisations;
2. Grasp the logic of corrective strategies within the realm of competition; and
3. Draw upon individual thinking and experiences to indicate the nature, scope and related issues concerning the possible network.

Formation of National Petroleum Management Programme (NPMP)

During the workshop, several managers said that a co-operative network can be detrimental to competitiveness. However, a majority of them felt that the nature of competition would depend on the kind of operations companies are engaged in. The competition will be less keen in the exploration and production business while companies engaged in marketing will face fierce competition. Competition will also differ among functions. Competition will be very high in the sales side and less in areas like finance, human resources, safety and effluent control. Based on theoretical analysis and international experience, it was felt that the future would see several co-operative strategies among progressive companies, even if they were competitors. Such co-operative moves will obviously require a sensitive and strategic analysis of areas of synergy, which will not have a net negative trade-off or create a conflict of strategic interests. It was recognised that there are substantial opportunities for leveraging inter-corporate capabilities for synergetic enhancement of competencies and efficiencies. Such possibilities exist through bilateral as well as multilateral co-operation.

The opportunities for co-operative moves range from the soft, non-strategic areas to the hard, strategic moves. In the latter, commitment of resources will be high, the strategic relevance for the corporations substantial, while the system of co-operation will be coupled with appropriate legal status and boundaries. The broad opportunities identified by the three working groups constituted in the workshop are:

- Functional meets across the oil industry for sharing of knowledge/experience;
- Inter-corporate HRD and skill upgradation (like vision workshops, petroleum management programmes, international trade, international finance, assimilation of new technologies/products);
- Inter-corporate information and knowledge sharing (illustratively in manual standardisation; sludge/effluent disposal; automation/computerisation; import substitution; gas utilisation; human resource redeployment; improvement in maintenance practices; disaster management; inter-sectoral awareness; customer orientation/service, etc.);
- Inter-corporate creative problem-solving exercises at strategic levels;
- Exchange of information on product, plant and environment standards and policies;
- Exchange of expertise/technology in select areas;
- Upgradation/sharing of communication networks;
- Mutually profitable utilisation of idle/surplus infrastructure facilities;
- Co-operative transfers of technology;
- Joint R&D, mutual access to specified facilities;
- Exchanging collaborative product transport/exchange;
- Coordinated import of crude;
- Consortia for turnkey contracts;
- Networking for finance requirement/clout, promotion of financial institutions;
- Acquiring marketing rights of private refineries;
- Launching of distribution companies; and
- New ventures in India and/or abroad through the joint venture corporation (JVC) route.

It was emphasised that there are eminent industry level organisations such as the Oil Co-ordination Committee (OCC), Centre for High Technology (CHT), Oil Industry Safety Directorate (OISD), Petroleum Conservation Research Association (PCRA), Petroleum India International (PII), and Petroleum Sector Control Board (PSCB). While some of these have been established through the joint initiative of the industry and the government, a few have been voluntary, industry-initiated efforts. These industry-level organisations have an important role in helping the petroleum industry, as well as the economy, and their missions and current activities are well focused. However, there are several more possibilities of co-operation, which may be complementary to these institutionalised networks. It was evident that some element of informal networking already existed but these were related to specific problems and tasks to facilitate smoother functioning at the operational levels, for example, crude/gas slate meeting, pipeline working group, lube group, liquefied petroleum gas (LPG) group, joint tenders for transport and port coordination.

Given the existing networks as well as the nature of the emerging competitive environment, combined with the availability of excellent internal capabilities, it was felt that there was a need to give a specific thrust to inter-corporate co-operation. This was based on the premise that though competition is inevitable, co-operative strategies would enhance the organisational capabilities/competence. This would lead, among other things, to organisational learning, timely strategic moves, enlarging strategic options, better leveraging of capabilities, warding off common threats and exploiting opportunities which would bring net positive pay-offs to the corporations, the economy as well as society at large. International research and experiments indicate that voluntarism is probably the best assurance of the vibrant functioning of any network. Also, while specific operating collaborations may be restricted to a few players with a lot in common, the fostering of co-operation among several companies may serve larger interests.

Based on all this, it was recommended that a voluntary body be established with the major objective of fostering co-operative strategies on a wide range of issues/activities. The membership of the forum can be open to existing, large manufacturing companies in the oil and petrochemical sector. It was decided to name this body the National Petroleum Management Programme (NPMP). The objectives of the NPMP as recommended in the workshop were defined as follows:

> NPMP is a voluntary, non-profit and consensus-driven body in pursuit of an outstanding record of demonstrable success in its goal-directed activities. NPMP is devoted to fostering co-operative networking among large companies in the oil, petroleum, petrochemicals and closely related businesses in India, for synergetic enhancement of their management, competencies and effectiveness. NPMP is guided by the philosophy that co-operative strategies are co-existential with competition, and that judicious and active co-operation would eventually lead to the welfare of the member companies as also the society at large. NPMP will facilitate the generation and transaction of visions, knowledge, analyses, information, perspectives and skills thus operating as a focal point for a wide range of strategic networking among member-companies.

Managing Organisational Change

Following the formation of NPMP, one of the primary thrust areas identified to develop a common strategy was to prepare the petroleum sector to recognise the global scenario and work out strategic directions for change. Competitive pressures will require a complete reorientation of the strategic thinking of oil companies. It was also recognised while there may be competition in certain areas, a lot of co-operative ventures among the oil companies to work out certain macro and micro level strategies were possible. It was decided to conduct a series of programmes on 'managing organisational change' for all levels of employees including collectives like trade unions and associations, middle level and senior level managers in collaboration with ASCI. The author was the main coordinator of the programme. As a prelude to these programmes, it was decided to initially interact with some of the global oil companies and management consultants dealing with the oil companies all over the world to see how the oil companies have been restructuring themselves to meet the competitive challenges. A seminar was organised in 1995 by the NPMP along with the OCC and the ministry of petroleum and natural gas. This was attended by policy makers from the government, board-level executives from the oil industry, key officials from international bodies, leading international consulting organisations and senior executives from state-owned oil companies in other countries as well as MNCs, who shared their experiences of successful restructuring programmes. It was decided to organise a series of follow-up programmes focusing on developing strategies and directions for changes at the enterprise level to meet the emerging challenges in the oil sector. The objectives of these programmes were:

- To sensitise the employees of the oil companies to the fast changing developments and key global trends in the petroleum industry;
- To enhance the understanding of complexities and dynamics of change facing the oil companies in achieving global competitive advantage; and
- To identify broad strategic directions for effectively managing change at the enterprise level.

Based on the detailed discussions in the NPMP workshop organised in 1993 and an international seminar in 1995, certain key strategic issues were identified which formed the basis for discussion in the series of workshops on managing organisational change. These issues are summarised as follows:

1. *The Enterprise in Transition*
   - Managing in the changing environment
   - Analyse the environment:
   — Necessity and willingness to change
   — Extent of change
   — What is the vision?

2. *Operational Strategies for Companies*
   - Communicating vision:
     — How do managers react?
     — What do workers think?
   - Analysing market and industry structures
   - Distribution and pricing—domestic and international
   - Addressing technology issues
   - Developing and implementing business plans
   - Refocusing competencies:
     — Which areas do you stay in?
     — Where do you diversify?
   - Focus on the customer:
     — How do you improve quality?
     — How do you make the customer paramount?

3. *Building Competitive Advantage in the Marketplace*
   - Strategies for developing core competencies
   - Gauging shifts in market competitiveness
   - Strategies for competing effectively in the international market place
   - Competitive advantage through information technology

4. *Organisational Structures*
   - Restructure the organisation
     — Can organisations be flattened?
     — How much more can the organisations pay?
     — Organising for market responsiveness
     — Addressing redundancy
     — Organisational alternatives
     — Managing information systems

5. *Human Resource Management*
   - Manpower planning, recruitment and training
   - Union/labour relations
   - Performance evaluation systems
   - Team building and conflict management
   - Employee shareholding plans

- Participative management
- Changing the mindset to accept changes

6. *Financing Enterprise*
   - Assessing financial needs
   - Sources of financing—domestic, foreign
   - Instruments for project financing

7. *Cost Engineering*
   - Estimating and controlling costs
   - Data management systems
   - Contingency management
   - Cost trending

8. *Establishing Strategic Alliances and Structuring Investment Agreements*
   - Restructure business
     — Who do you tie up with?
     — Who do you buy up?
     — How do you go global?
   - Establishing alliances with suppliers, distributors and customers
   - Investment agreements with local and foreign companies

9. *Making Sound Investment Decisions*
   - Identifying viable projects and product lines
   - Strategic partnership analysis
   - Evaluating investments
   - Capital budgeting considerations
   - Valuation methodology

10. *Effective Financial Management*
    - Restructure finance
    - Assessing business performance
    - Inventory management
    - Accounting policies
    - Analysing financial statements

- Liquidity, debt and asset management
- Cash flow
- How to strengthen the financial controls?

11. *Restructuring Production*
    - How does one automate?
    - Can shop-floor teams be created?
    - Business process re-engineering

12. *Government–Industry Relations*
    - Supervision, taxation and regulation
    - Post-privatisation, role of government and industry
    - Functioning of memorandums of understanding (MUs) with the government

All these above issues were clubbed into five broad themes. These were:

1. Enterprise-in-transition;
2. Building competitive advantage;
3. Organisational restructuring and HRM;
4. Financial management; and
5. Technology transfer, assimilation and upgradation.

Four programmes were conducted for various levels of employees. The first two programmes were conducted for middle level managers of the oil sector. The third programme was specifically for representatives of the trade unions and the officers' associations and the fourth programme was for the board-level directors including the chief executives of these companies. Some of the salient points on the strategic directions made by different levels of employees are given below.

Salient Points Made by Managers

Environment
- Increasing dependence on imports of petroleum products is affecting India's economy;

- Need for export orientation to reduce the import burden;
- Need to maximise India's share in global reserves;
- Opening up of the economy;
- Increase in external and internal competition by allowing domestic private firms and MNCs into the petroleum sector;
- Establishment of joint ventures with private players and MNCs;
- Opening up of the lube sector;
- Pricing decontrol, assuming one of the following scenarios:
  — a completely decontrolled environment
  — gradual decontrol
  — continuation of APM for a few more years;
- Possibility of crude price decontrol;
- Possibility of ex-refinery price decontrol;
- Decontrol of free trade products;
- Parallel marketing decontrol;
- Tariff reduction on petroleum products;
- Parallel marketing of kerosene/LPG/low sulphur heavy stocks (LSHS);
- Direct import by end-users of naptha, LSHS/aviation turbine fuel (ATF)/fuel oil/bitumen, etc.;
- Only crude, motor spirit (MS), high speed diesel (HSD) now under canalisation;
- Need for public sector oil companies to go through prudential supervision as they have to fend for themselves in the absence of APM;
- Stringent environment regulations regarding oil spills, gas flaring and lead emission; and
- Infrastructure inadequacies, e.g., port congestion.

Vision

- Development of specific vision and goals;
- 'Globally integrated Indian multinational corporation at par with other global players with diverse activities in petroleum, oil and lubricants (POL) and related fields across the world by 2010';

- For developing a broad-based vision, the following need to be considered:
  — Potential for growth in the existing business within the country
  — Potential for being a global player for growth
  — Diversification in related areas for growth
  — Developing competitive edge in quality, customer service, price and loyalty of employees towards the company;
- Vision to be communicated and made acceptable to most of the employees;
- Share major challenges and information regarding competition; and
- Have video programmes on international experiences.

Strategies

Building Competitive Advantage
- Consolidate core competencies;
- Identify areas of diversification and integration;
- Offer customer happiness (not just satisfaction) through low cost, high quality, utmost safety and quality service;
- Effective R&D to gain competitive advantage;
- Continuous marketing research/feedback and creative action. A central body to initiate and monitor such steps is necessary;
- Strategic alliances among public, private and multinational oil companies;
- Shift emphasis from distribution and logistics to marketing; and
- Strive for a common approach by oil companies to meet global competition by identifying areas and modalities of co-operation.

Organisation, Restructuring and HRM
- Maximisation of value of human resources as part of the mission;
- Changes and adjustments in mindset and attitude, recognising the new realities;
- Lean, mean and flat organisational structure;
- Appropriate investment in HRD through proper and relevant training needs identification;
- Appropriate review of systems and procedures to get optimum contribution from human resources;
- Develop plans for empowering people and training them;

- Identify surplus and shortages among staff and develop redeployment and training strategies;
- Appropriate placement of personnel based on their interests and aptitudes;
- Offer VRS with caution;
- Full utilisation of computers and other IT facilities and training personnel in their use; and
- Developing participatory institutions.

Finance
- Mobilisation of resources through disinvestment;
- Investment strategy:
  — areas of core competence to be thrust areas
  — minimum 15 per cent post-tax returns on new investments
  — adopting joint venture route
  — major investments in technology for long-term benefit
- Funding strategy:
  — debt/equity ratio can be 3:1
  — internal generation of funds
  — borrowing options can be either from domestic market or foreign market, or both
  — equity option offering to local/foreign shareholders
  — Venture route in the present fast changing environment
- Control measures
  — adopting a profit centre concept
  — motivating through an effective modern project/construction management system
  — effective liquidity/asset/inventory/debt management
  — strengthen financial control through strict budget review
  — minimise financial risk by appropriate hedging/swapping

Technology
- Commitment of the top management towards R&D;
- Draw up a short-term and long-term R&D and technology policy;
- Foster an attitudinal change towards R&D;
- Strategic alliance with other R&D centres for scientific as well as business research;
- Involvement of R&D personnel in the acquisition/transfer/ assimilation/upgradation of technology;

- Due to resource constraints, heavy investment in R&D and technology development is not possible. There is need for strategic alliances with MNCs for technology transfers;
- Developing technology requires long gestation periods. Therefore, there is need to concentrate on selected core areas, reverse engineering, and breakthrough technology;
- Automation in installation of LPG/lubes, etc.,
- Develop pipeline networking;
- New product formulation;
- Exploration—develop state-of-the-art technology for seismic studies, well logging and exploitation of enhanced oil recovery;
- Exploit the benefits of horizontal drilling;
- Product quality improvement and reduction in cost:
  — development of separation technology
  — residue upgradation
  — developing technology of lube, bitumen and petrochemical
  — minimising loss control
  — avoiding pollution
  — promoting energy conservation
  — improving on steam factor
  — production of high value products
  — advanced control
- Think of future technologies, such as:
  — microbial organisms
  — biodegradable products
  — new generation hydrocarbons
- Process and product re-engineering to reduce cost and improve efficiency.

Salient Points Made by Collectives (Trade Unions and Officers' Associations)

Restructuring and Human Resource Management

- Vision of self-sufficiency to be achieved through internal efficiencies, increase in production and export of petroleum products to earn foreign exchange, in order to buy more crude;

- Involvement of employees in vision formulation and implementation strategies;
- More commercialisation of the enterprise and leaving the board to take decisions regarding technology, location of plants, expansions, etc., so long as they generate internal resources for expansion;
- Decisions to be made by the person on the spot. It should be referred to a higher level only when it involves some value addition. Hence, people at various levels should be adequately empowered;
- Presently there are too many layers and also lack of role clarity;
- Surplus staff to be trained and redeployed after assessing manpower requirements in the present scenario;
- Employee performance evaluation is subjective. Some measurable yardsticks need to be developed to enhance objectivity;
- Group performance assessment to be introduced;
- The methodology of training needs identification to be improved;
- Training to be based on skill requirements for the organisation irrespective of the level/function;
- An environment to improve team building be created. This can be done by:
  — improving the internal communications system
  — monthly departmental meeting at all levels
  — increasing informal interactions
  — quick redressal of grievances; and
- Institutionalised joint decision-making process is necessary.

Building Competitive Advantage
- Core competencies to be built upon to give competitive advantage;
- Areas of diversification to be identified and built upon;
- Identify export markets and increase exports, thereby improving foreign exchange position;
- Joint ventures with other public sector companies, private and foreign companies to synergise the efforts of all.

The following hurdles need to be removed:
— fear of take-over by MNCs
— non-sharing of information with employees regarding joint ventures
— disincentive for internal technological development
— problem of compensation differential due to joint ventures;
- Minimise cost and be cost competitive by:
— introducing e-mail
— streamlining purchase procedures systems
— improvement in inventory control;
- Financial control to be exercised and cost effective decisions rather than low cost decisions to be taken and timely payment to suppliers made;
- Vigilance at outlets regarding product/brand to prevent spurious products; and
- Corporate image enhancement to sell own products/brands.

Customer Orientation
- Ensure product availability at all locations;
- Freedom to select retail outlets/distributors;
- Develop information network of markets;
- Customer service and satisfaction;
- Customer surveys on quality, quantity and service;
- Training to all employees, dealers and distributors;
- Amenities at service points and outlets; and
- Prompt redressal of customer complaints.

Technology
- Thrust to be given to R&D;
- Concentration needed in the following areas:
— optimisation of operations
— reducing pollution
— energy conservation;
- Automation through IT;
- Re-engineering and systems improvement;
- Training and development of personnel in new technologies;
- A clear policy for technology transfer, assimilation and upgradation;

- Joint action by public sector oil companies to face global competition. They can pool their resources and develop the latest technology; and
- Develop a total quality management (TQM) culture by:
  — maintaining the ISO 9000 standards
  — bringing R&D activities on par with international standards.

Salient Points Made by Directors

The final programme for the directors was organised to discuss the recommendations of the earlier programmes, with a view to developing strategic directions and leadership action at all levels for initiating and managing organisational change. Some of the salient points made were:

Restructuring and HRM
- A strategy needs to be worked out to implement all the suggestions made in the earlier programmes. This will necessitate certain actions by top management, collectives and government officials;
- Overall review of the organisational structures and broad policies may be needed in view of the changed competitive environment;
- The bottom line approach or, the profit centre concept needs to be adopted;
- Core areas and service factors can be identified and a methodology to synergise be worked out. The top management has to be the main change agents;
- Determine the size of the organisation and redeploy surplus employees after training them;
- The public sector is overstaffed but terminating an employee's services is very difficult. The VRS scheme has not been of much use since the efficient employees opt for it;
- Develop ancillary industries to utilise part of the surplus manpower, wherever necessary;
- There are many layers and little specialisation. It is necessary to introduce multi-skilling, reduce the number of layers and introduce the system of planned job rotation;

- Environmental concerns need to be addressed;
- IT facilities must be better utilised;
- Benchmarking by identifying the best practices in the industry across countries;
- The top management spends a lot of time in providing data and information to the government and in reality very little of such data is used;
- The efficiency of public sector enterprises will improve with the dismantling of the APM. However, it was noted that it is the new private players who are asking for APM as a protective mechanism;
- Knowledge is a powerful tool today. Hence, all employees need to be trained in the latest developments;
- The unions and associations should be exposed to international experience by arranging visits to foreign refineries;
- A framework for developing professionally qualified managers as future leaders has to be created;
- Sharing of information is extremely important. Employees need to be informed about all major issues. For example, they need to be informed about joint ventures and the areas of agreement with the other company;
- There is also a need to have a dialogue with employees on all organisational matters;
- The top management has to clearly define the extent of sharing of information with employees;
- Interpersonal relations need to be improved;
- Personal interactions need to be increased;
- Delegating and empowerment is a key factor in decision making. Empowerment should be understood in the sense of making one capable of dealing with day-to-day problems;
- Cultural change needs to be emphasised more than systems change. At present there appears to be a dependency culture where no responsibility is taken for the output. A risk taking culture needs to be developed.
- Decision making should be done at different levels and the decisions referred to the next level must involve some value addition;

- A fast track promotion channel must be adopted for the professionally qualified and excellent performers. Promotion has to be pursued as a reward, for which other factors like placing an individual in the area of his/her expertise, interest have to be considered; and
- Right now, promotions are the only reward to motivate people; as a result, a lot of people are promoted which necessitates the recruitment of people at lower levels leading to surplus manpower. A re-look at the promotional policy is necessary. There is also a need to find other ways of motivating people.

Technology
- There is a need to bring in the latest technology from outside and also develop technology within;
- Wider spectrum of technologies is creating a problem. Interchanging the manpower among the various levels of technologies is not accompanied by sufficient training;
- Technology can also be used to improve the existing product; and
- A long-term policy of technology transfer, assimilation and upgradation for each organisation is necessary.

Cost Minimisation
- Cost cutting will help the organisation improve profitability. However, cost reductions must be distinguished from expenditure reductions;
- In most projects there are delays and demands for additional resources. There is a need for better planning in project management to ensure adequate returns in the competitive environment; and
- Port capacity needs to be managed in a better way to minimise costs.

While summing up the series of programmes, the secretary, ministry of petroleum and natural gas, made the following observations:

- There is a need to stick to core competencies rather than diversify into unrelated areas;

- MNCs should not be perceived as a threat but as an opportunity for the public sector enterprises to grow by taking advantage of the new technologies and better utilisation of available, existing skills;
- Exposing the enterprises to the global environment will result in cheaper availability of foreign capital for investment in India;
- Companies need to make adjustments—alliances, mergers and capital restructuring;
- Public sector oil companies still have a feudal culture; they need to change their mindset;
- With public sector enterprises going in for joint ventures, various internal policies, including compensation packages, need to be reviewed;
- The government is gradually giving more autonomy to the public sector enterprises but since it continues to be the major shareholder, the management must learn to live with government supervision. The board of directors must educate bureaucrats about areas in which they need more autonomy;
- The government has already taken steps to get all new proposals vetted by financial institutions and not necessarily by government officials;
- The board of directors must concentrate on developing long term strategies for change rather than on day-to-day operational issues;
- There is a need for internal operational efficiencies including cost reduction and better financial and management technique. There is always a risk of failure; the board should provide for this, as is the pattern in many large international companies; and
- A programme can be organised for the members of the parliamentary consultative committee on petroleum and the advisory committee of the ministry of petroleum to sensitise them to the various challenges and issues concerning the sector.

From the recommendations made by different groups, it is evident that there is convergence of views on the challenges being faced by the oil sector. There was a broad consensus that all the companies will have to work out certain common macro-level as well as enterprise-level strategies to prepare themselves for change. In the initial stages, the managers as well as the collectives expressed the fear that there may be clash of interest between these two groups. However, it was heartening to note that there was no marked differences of views and, in fact, there were large areas of commonalties and this can be a positive point to work out common strategies for the future.

Follow-up Steps

One of the strategic directions which emerged was that each organisation will need to work out short- and long-term strategies in the following broad areas:

- Developing a long-term shared vision and also preparing operational strategies for communicating this vision and getting it accepted by employees at all levels;
- Gauging shifts in market competitiveness and developing strategies for core competencies;
- Restructuring the organisation for market responsiveness;
- Concentrate on HRD, especially training employees for new technology;
- Developing competitive advantage through IT;
- Reviewing the employee performance evaluation system to bring in a developmental orientation;
- Developing better financial and cost control measures;
- Working out R&D and technology strategies for technology transfer, assimilation and upgradation;
- The recommendations made in the various programmes on 'managing organisational change' have been very exhaustive but at the same time these were obviously general because of the heterogeneous nature of the groups, with members drawn from different sectors and different companies. There is an urgent need to make appropriate changes in the recommendations, specific to each organisation. In other words, enterprise-

level strategies need to be worked out. Companies need to adapt these recommendations to their own specific contexts;

- A mass movement by officers' associations, trade unions and the management is necessary as there is a commonalty on most issues;
- There is a need to involve middle and junior level employees in the process of managing organisational change. A series of case studies for middle and junior management can yield a lot of benefits and it can also have a multiplier effect;
- For a greater acceptance by employees, the top management has to sustain its efforts in being transparent and consistent;
- The topic of 'managing change' must be a part of all training programmes; and
- At the macro level there is need for companies to come together in certain areas and develop joint strategies for common infrastructure development.

At the end of the programme, there was a broad consensus that each enterprise will set up task forces to work out enterprise-level strategies on the recommendations. It was also agreed that another programme be held after some time to discuss the implementation of these recommendations and develop further strategies.

In conclusion, it is a unique experience where a set of competing organisations have come together through a networking system—the NPMP—by which they are able to work out certain common strategies. A beginning has already been made when four major oil companies combined to form a holding company—Petronet India Ltd—to promote JVs to set up pipelines in the country. It is yet to be seen how effective this experiment will be. It is perceived to be helpful to all the organisations to not only compete effectively in the global market, but also work out certain strategies which will help them to prepare for change.

Index